THE WAY OF POWERLESSNESS
Advaita and the Twelve Steps of Recovery

Advaita Press

Also by
Wayne (Ram Tzu) Liquorman:

NO WAY for the Spiritually "Advanced"

Acceptance of What IS...a book about Nothing

Never Mind

Enlightenment is Not What You Think

THE WAY OF POWERLESSNESS

Advaita and the Twelve Steps of Recovery

By Wayne Liquorman

Edited by Dawn Salva

Published in the USA by

Advaita Press
PO Box 3479
Redondo Beach, CA 90277
Tel: 310-376-9636
Email: fellowship@advaita.org
www.advaita.org

Cover and Interior Design: Tara Scarcello
Cover Photo: Chris Redmond
Rear Cover Photo: Gayle Goodrich

ISBN: 978-0-929448-25-1

Library of Congress Control Number: 2012946089

Dedicated to the men at Scotty's/Splash.
Who showed me how to live in Peace
Which is what I was looking for all along...

In all the wrong places.

I'm just another miracle
A common resurrection
Lifted out of the dead zone
Into the light.
–Wayne
First week of sobriety.
June 1985

CONTENTS

Sharing Our Experience
The Wave is the Ocean

DEAR READER,

I sit here trying to imagine you as you open this book and read these words. I see you as either a spiritual seeker (already familiar with the basic nondual perspective of Advaita) or someone pursuing the path of recovery through one of the many Twelve Step programs. Whether you are one of these things, or both, or neither, I welcome you to what I hope will be a pleasant and enlightening journey. As journeys go it is an unusual one in that no matter how long it lasts or how difficult it may sometimes be, the final destination is always right where you are.

That you have even picked this book up makes you something of an oddity. I wonder what has happened to you to make you susceptible to the possibility that powerlessness could be the key to something beneficial?

Powerlessness! On the surface it seems a horrible word pointing to an even less desirable condition. It is nearly synonymous with death, the ultimate condition of powerlessness. Most societies treat powerlessness as an illness, something to be treated and overcome.

If you are anything like I was upon encountering the idea of powerlessness, you feel that the answer to life's problems lies in gaining *more* power, not in having less.

The proposition that lasting peace in life can come only through the recognition of complete personal powerlessness seems, on the surface, to be counterintuitive and ultimately ridiculous. Yet, discovering the freedom available through the recognition of your own complete personal powerlessness is what this book is all about.

I was first introduced to the notion of peace through personal powerlessness in the Twelve Steps of Alcoholics Anonymous. Later I found this very same principle in the nondual spiritual teachings of Taoism, Zen, Sufism and Advaita, as well as many of the mystic writings of Judaism and Christianity. In other words, this is hardly a new idea, though throughout human history it has never been a very readily accepted one. We will explore the reasons why personal powerlessness is so difficult for most people to accept as we go forward.

If you find yourself sufficiently empowered to go on reading this book, you may be surprised to discover that you have actually been powerless all along. You may begin to see that your suffering in life is a direct result of the FALSE sense that you have the power to control. As you awaken to the recognition of what is True about yourself and the world around you, you begin to live in harmony with yourself and with others. With Grace, you will awaken to a vision of life as it actually is and discover the Peace that inevitably accompanies this vision.

May it find you now.

Wayne Liquorman
Hermosa Beach, California
July 2012

EDITOR'S NOTE

If I had the power, I would declare *The Way of Power-lessness* mandatory reading for any adult who ever encounters another person in any way, shape or form, especially those that encounter me! But, as I have no such power, not even the power to control myself, I know it is unlikely the world will cooperate. Yet, I still hope there is something I can do that will create immediate and great interest in this book. The seeming contradiction between knowing there is great power, and recognizing personal powerlessness is exactly what *The Way of Powerlessness* brilliantly reconciles.

I had no idea how much I would fall in love with this book. When Wayne first mentioned it, I wasn't even remotely interested in the Twelve Steps. Even after I began working on it with him, I had no idea what a profound and beautiful impact this book would have on my life. For that, I am eternally grateful to Wayne and to Source.

I remain astounded that although I can name several personal addictions from both the past and present, I never considered myself in need of the Steps. Nor did I realize how my own compulsions and addictions (both in deed and thought) could be the avenue for a deepening of spiritual understanding.

Addiction is a surprisingly fertile place to look for spiritual insight, particularly if one is blessed with a moment of clarity and/or recovery. We are fortunate to have Wayne as a loving, humorous and ever so engrossing Guide. His pure compassion, his ability to undermine false perception and his Ultimate Understanding radiate in this book. It is like he is reaching out and saying, "Come take my hand, I'll walk with you." And, through the Living Teaching in this book, he does.

Framing Advaita in the Twelve Steps, (or is it the other way around?) was no small feat. Harnessing the incomprehensible power of powerlessness into words is ultimately impossible. But the words in this book aren't mere concepts. Instead, they are potent pointers to where and how to look at the most accessible doorway to spiritual understanding — ourselves.

Whether you are simply curious, or a spiritual seeker, or find this book in your hands because of your exposure to the Twelve Steps, it is Grace that brings you here. The Wisdom contained within these pages has no boundaries and will keep giving, guiding and loving for long after you put this volume back on the shelf.

Dawn Salva
July 2012

THE TWELVE STEPS

I love the Twelve Steps of Alcoholics Anonymous. They are as beautiful to me as any great work of art. They have introduced me to a way to live comfortably in my own skin, as I am in this moment, a collection of characteristics both admirable and defective. There is nothing in the world quite like them.

These twelve deceptively simple Steps contain within them a blueprint for living with What Is, one day at a time. By "What Is" I mean life as it is actually happening, rather than our opinion of how life "should" be. The Steps have also been known to lead to a spiritual awakening that brings a Peace beyond all human understanding.

As befits something that is so important to so many people, much has been written about the Twelve Steps. Although I despair of being able to add anything new and meaningful to the discussion, I have lived intimately with these Steps for a long time now and the itch has come to write about them from the perspective of my other role as a teacher of Advaita (an ancient branch of Hinduism that points to the Unity of all things, also known as nondualism). For those of you who do not know what Advaita or nondualism is — not to worry — they are neither as esoteric nor as daunting as they may sound. In fact, you may realize that you already know what these terms point to; you just didn't have a name for it. Through the course of this book you may also discover that both Advaita and the Twelve Steps point to a single, very simple and basic Truth — as individuals we are totally and completely powerless.

By the way, you are free to disagree with this assertion at this point. In fact, I hope you will test everything I say. Certainly on the surface it appears that we do have power. But when you look more deeply, you may come to realize that whatever power you exercise comes from a power greater than the egoic self. In other words, there is power, but it isn't truly yours. It is given to you, on loan. Who or What this power greater than the "egoic self" is may not be readily apparent. Both the Twelve Steps and Advaita are tools to aid in the process of discovering the profound depth of this power greater than the personal self.

Since the writing of the book Alcoholics Anonymous (affectionately known as the Big Book) in 1939, the Steps contained therein have been applied to aid recovery from a wide range of other types of addictions as well. One of the key components of this program, arguably "THE" key component, is the recognition of personal powerlessness; first regarding the substance or behavior causing you a problem in life, and finally, regarding EVERYTHING.

Power, control, and self-discipline. These are the holy trinity of human desire. Deluded by the fantasy that such things are attainable, we believe that when attained, we will be able to create whatever we want and life will be perfect. The Big Book does not support this premise. It speaks to the fact that we are undisciplined so "we let God discipline us."[1] It then goes on to suggest we are powerless and cannot manage (control) our lives and that recognizing this is the key to true strength. It thus flies in the face of conventional human wisdom. I never cease to be amazed that such a bold expression of powerlessness exists, much less flourishes in the way it does today in the many Twelve Step programs.

Addicts, compulsives and certain spiritual seekers have something surprising in common. They all share an amazing potential to see through the illusion of their own personal power. This potential arises out of their life experience in which they continually find themselves acting on an irresistible urge to do something they know will ultimately bring them problems.

ANONYMITY

A word about anonymity. Alcoholics Anonymous and its many offshoots are all anonymous programs. This means that the members of these programs are enjoined to maintain personal anonymity at the public level. It is a venerable tradition and one that has many practical benefits. Accordingly, I make no claim to membership in any of the Twelve Step programs, though as you will soon see, I certainly qualify for several.

Please allow me to introduce myself... I'm a pig. Perhaps not a very active one these days, but from the age of sixteen till I was thirty-five, my primary mission in life was to get MORE. MORE applied to everything I liked and what I liked best was drugs and alcohol. I did a lot of both. It was as if there was a giant hole in me that I tried desperately to fill. Sometimes I got enough and the hole filled to the brim for a blissful moment of satisfaction and peace. But the hole had a leak at the bottom. Whatever I put in it was quickly gone. I was always left feeling empty again, desperate for MORE. The ongoing misery of my life was that MORE never proved to be enough.

At the end of the active phase of my alcoholism and drug addiction, my once successful business was failing. My marriage was dead (though we were dancing hopefully around the corpse). I was unable to show up physically or emotionally for my wife and my two young children. My health deteriorated to the point that my ankles and wrists were swollen with alcoholic edema. I lost fine control of my bladder so that I had to stuff a wad of toilet paper down my pants to catch a minute but constant leak of urine. This improvised diaper required changing every half hour or so. I spent as many hours of the day as possible in my local bar. I began my day in the late morning with rum in my coffee to stop the shakes and a line of cocaine to "get alert." Each morning when I tried to brush my teeth, I had the dry heaves on my toothbrush.

I tell you this only so that when I say that my attitude was, "I'm fine, I don't have a problem. Sure, I enjoy drinking and doing drugs, but I have it all under control," you will understand I was in total denial. I was literally crumbling inward, but I couldn't see it. I had no desire to get sober and besides, THERE WAS NO NEED FOR IT! I was FINE! Furthermore, I couldn't stand to be around people who didn't drink and do drugs. They clearly had no idea what high quality life was all about as they lived their boring, sober little lives. The very last thing on earth I wanted to be was one of THEM.

People often say that the only prerequisite for sobriety is willingness. That may be true, but in my case anyway, I am certain that it wasn't "my" willingness. In fact, my wants, my desires, and my willingness had absolutely nothing to do with the two most dramatic turning points in my life (as I will describe shortly). In my experience, the only prerequisite for recovery is Grace, though I am actually more comfortable saying, recovery IS Grace. This beautiful word, Grace, is defined in the dictionary as: Unmerited favor from God.

"Unmerited" meaning that I did nothing to earn or deserve it. "Favor" meaning that the result was something ultimately positive. "From God" meaning that some force in the Universe, other than an independent and powerful "me," was responsible for bringing it about.

THE FIRST AWAKENING
(to the possibility that I wasn't in control)

It was the end of a long, Memorial Day weekend in 1985. I was very drunk and very high on cocaine, but it was not a "fun" high, it was a "sick" high. I had been up for days and all I wanted was to go to sleep. I tried smoking some very powerful pot and drinking straight rum with the hope of passing out, but it didn't work. I lay in bed sweating and tossing and turning. Suddenly and without warning I was stone, cold sober. I had the curious sensation of something leaving my body. I felt it go, but didn't realize until later that it was the obsession that had been part of me for nineteen years vacating my body. All I knew at the time was that something in me had radically changed — and I must say I wasn't happy about it. A deep part of me knew that it was over, that I wasn't going to be able to continue with my life as I knew it. I was scared to death. Even though it was one in the morning, I was wide-awake and painfully sober.

I knew nothing about AA nor had I ever been to one of their meetings, but it suddenly occurred to me that I should call Alcoholics Anonymous and turn myself in to them. I called and despite the hour, someone picked up the phone. I asked him when their next meeting was and he gave me an address for a meeting at 7AM.

For the next five hours I threw myself a "going away" party. I endeavoured to get every last bit of drugs and alcohol remaining in the house into my body. True to form, I figured if I was going out, I was going out with a bang! I sat at my dining room table swilling straight liquor and snorting barely chopped cocaine... big rocks of it falling out of my nose and bouncing onto the floor. I remained maddeningly sober.

Despite not having slept or bathed for days, I went to the 7AM meeting. I did not identify myself as a newcomer, yet somehow it seemed they were able to figure it out. All in all, I remember it as a horrible experience; sick early morning light filtered in through the louvered windows illuminating the floating dust motes. Squeaky clean looking people sat on metal folding chairs arranged in a circle talking altogether too much about God. One woman was even talking about driving the church school bus! I had secretly suspected my life would eventually come to this.

It was as if I had used up my quota of fun (if you call peeing in your pants fun) and now I would have to endure the rest of my days in prissy, lifeless gatherings such as this. Had I any better options, I would have taken them.

I left that first meeting with two things that turned out to be treasures. One was a directory of all the meetings in the area (some of which I discovered were much more lively and to my taste) and the other was the Big Book of AA[2] containing the Twelve Steps. In that moment, I couldn't have possibly imagined how significant those Steps would be in the months and years to come, or how my life was about to change even more dramatically.

In the following pages I will endeavour to share my personal relationship with the Twelve Steps. However, I must emphasize that I am neither a spokesman nor an authority. I don't believe there is a single way to approach the Steps, just as there is no single way to pray or meditate. Part of the splendour of the Steps is their simplicity and their universality. They can work for anyone regardless of gender, religion, race, culture, nationality or history. You need not have lived an exemplary life. You need not believe in God or have any other type of spiritual understanding. In fact, in my opinion (and I assure you many people will disagree) there are absolutely NO prerequisites. This means you can approach the Steps from wherever you are in this moment. Sinner? You are in good company. Liar? Cheat? All are welcome. Selfish? Self-centered? Obsessed? Come on in. You'll feel right at home.

A note: Although alcohol and cocaine brought me to the Steps; the Steps, while alcohol specific in language, are not alcohol specific in application. Throughout the book, please feel free to substitute alcohol with the substance or behavior that disrupted your own life enough for you to read it.

This is also probably a good time to point out that the Steps were written by Christian men inspired by the Four Practices of the Oxford Group, an early twentieth century Christian religious movement. Much of the language and tone of the Steps and the Big Book reflects this bias. What makes the Twelve Steps unique is that they are elastic, spacious and non-dogmatic. There is a natural and appealing humility about them. They are unquestionably spiritual in nature, but it is a free and open spirituality. They are not bound by any particular religion. They make no claim to "divine inspiration" and assert no moral absolute. This absence of dogma and moral righteousness is reassuring for people like me who come to the Steps agnostic and morally bankrupt. After all, it is hard to argue with people that say in their book, "We realize we know only a little."[3]

The subject of personal powerlessness is also central to the spiritual teaching of nondualism called Advaita. Advaita, a Sanskrit word meaning "not two," describes an ancient Teaching pointing to the underlying Unity of all things.

The two strong influences of the Twelve Steps and Advaita have run parallel in my life for more than twenty-five years. Finally the urge has come to bring them together. This book is an attempt to do just that.

Ultimately, the Steps are about looking deeply into what is True. When engaged in rigorously, such looking WILL be uncomfortable since the Steps push you out of your comfort zone. With Grace, you will be pushed out of your familiar nest and into a freefall that is mystical Understanding — conceptless, open and free. It is a space of infinite potential in which you know yourself as BOTH the Limitless and the limited.

May it find you now.

ADVAITA

I love Advaita. It is as beautiful to me as any great work of art. It has given me a way to live comfortably in my own skin, as I am in this moment, a collection of characteristics both admirable and defective. There is nothing in the world quite like it.

If you are already familiar with the Steps, but not with Advaita, you may be quite surprised at how the understanding of powerlessness in Advaita mirrors what is pointed to in the Steps. If you are a student of Advaita, but not yet exposed to the Steps, you may discover in them some practices that may fuel your understanding of the essence of powerlessness. If you have no knowledge of either the Twelve Steps or of Advaita, hold on tight, you are in for a wild ride!

As I mentioned previously, I am a teacher in the Advaita tradition of nondualism. As such, I have travelled the world since 1997 talking to groups of interested people about Consciousness, God, Source, Higher Power, Totality...call It whatever you like. I suppose you could say my job description is Spiritual Teacher or Guru (a once highly respected term, now often used with a disparaging sneer).

How this came to be is beyond improbable. If anyone requires evidence that we are not the creators of our own destinies, my life offers ample proof.

Suffice it to say, as I sat for endless hours in the bar watching reruns of old football games, itching to place bets on them, my hopes and dreams never wandered to the idea that I might someday write books about Consciousness and travel the world as a teacher of personal powerlessness, welcomed into people's lives and homes in such diverse places as Spain, Russia, India, Sweden, Turkey and Australia (to name but a few). Such a possibility was far, far beyond imagining. Furthermore, even after I became sober and developed an interest in the possibilities of personal powerlessness, it never occurred to me to be a teacher, much less a "Guru." I was perfectly content to be a husband, father and businessman. But the Universe clearly had other plans.

THE SECOND AWAKENING
(leading to the Living Teaching)

In 1989, the sense that I was a separate, independent entity with the power to author my own thoughts, feelings and actions died completely within "me," the entity known as Wayne Liquorman. This so-called event marked the end of any possibility of suffering happening through me since, as you may soon see, suffering is directly tied to the sense of being an independent, powerful entity. To a few people (sometimes called spiritual seekers) this makes me interesting, desirable and worth sitting around with, regardless of whether I talk or not.

I must quickly add that this occurrence did not turn me into a Saint. A Saint is someone whose behavior embodies the highest ideals of a group. My behavior, before and after this "second awakening," doesn't represent the highest ideals of any group and though I am no longer much of a betting man, I would be willing to bet that it never will. I am completely ordinary in all significant categories of behavior. But in the words of the Big Book, I am no longer "a victim of the delusion that he can wrest satisfaction and happiness out of this world if he only manages well."[4] I am completely convinced of my own powerlessness and my life flows accordingly, sometimes calmly, sometimes turbulently, but always grounded in underlying Peace.

This Peace came with the recognition of my complete and utter powerlessness. It is a Peace that surpasses all understanding; which is to say that it is not conditional, it is transcendent. It is there regardless of surface calmness or turbulence. All is understood to be happening perfectly, even if in the moment I don't like it. There is total acceptance of What Is in this moment.

From the outside I look and act like most everyone else, while inside I am transformed. Not into something special, but into That which we have always been.

Advaita, as it came to me and as I now teach it, is a collection of pointers designed to encourage an investigation into who and what we truly are. I call it The Living Teaching. It is without precept or dogma and makes no claims or promises. It exists only to facilitate a spiritual quest and to keep it open to new possibilities. The Living Teaching asks questions rather than answers them, since the right question at the right moment can push us beyond what we believe into directly seeing That which is always here. As such, everything is included; nothing is excluded in the Living Teaching.

The Living Teaching is concerned with the living energy that is here now, expressing itself as us, and through us, as life itself. It points to the fact that each of us is a movement of this Life Force playing out as living experience through our minds and bodies. It hopes to foster the understanding that the experience of living is itself, spiritual. Recognizing this may require a radical expansion of your definition of spiritual. Most people tend to associate spiritual with only "good" things. Things we think are nice, kind, loving and gentle, we say are spiritual. Things we think harsh, constricted, ugly and unpleasant, we say are un-spiritual, or material. This thinking is quite engrained in most of us. With Grace, we may be able to get past this limited perspective and expand to realize that what we all are, what everything is, is Spiritual. The greatest challenge is always to see the bad and the painful as Spiritual too.

If all of that sounds pretty esoteric and obscure (and full of too many words with Capital Letters) it probably is. Ultimately, all the words and descriptions don't really matter. Intellectually understanding the descriptions is the consolation prize. My hope as a facilitator of both the Living Teaching and the Twelve Steps, is that reading this book will help the process of intuitive knowing unfold within you, ultimately bringing more peace to your life through the direct recognition of who and what you truly Are.

May it find you now.

LIQUORMAN

OK, let's get this out of the way. Yes, I was born with the name Wayne Liquorman and from the age of 16 until I was 35 I did everything in my power to live up to it. That nearly killed me, but I am happy to report that, as of this writing, I am very much alive. Alive in a way I never could have imagined. Alive in a way I find very difficult to describe. I am completely ordinary and yet all that I think, feel and do is beyond extraordinary. What I once considered ordinary today is miraculous. I find it miraculous that I am able to take this breath, the oxygen of which transfers to my blood carrying it to every part of my body, enabling me to have this thought and write these words. It is miraculous that I can feel the pain of others and care what happens to someone else. It is miraculous that the irresistible compulsion to drink alcohol and use drugs was removed and remains gone. It is miraculous that this entity called Wayne lives as an integral part of All That Is without any sense of having personal power.

For me today, the ordinary and the extraordinary are one and the same thing, as are the spiritual and the material, as are me and the other. I consider this intuitive recognition of the "One in the many" to be the spiritual awakening spoken of both in the Twelve Steps and in Advaita.

May it find you now.

STEP ONE

"We admitted we were powerless over alcohol—
that our lives had become unmanageable."

The essence of the First Step is powerlessness. We are powerless over ____ (feel free to fill in the blank with whatever fits) and our lives are unmanageable — presumably by us. That we might actually be powerless over something is the crack in the wall that lets some light in. At first, it is often only a single ray of light, but it enables us to glimpse the Truth that is here, right now.

The Steps introduce the notion of powerlessness slowly. The entry point is our personal experience of being powerless over whatever it is that brings us to the Steps.

Step One doesn't try to convince us of anything. On the contrary, it simply points us to look at our own experience. After all, if we had power over ____ we wouldn't be here in the first place. Right? The Big Book is so adamant about this recognition of powerlessness that it says if you aren't absolutely convinced that you are powerless over it (whatever "it" is) then go ahead and try to control it. Test this assumption of personal power within yourself. Powerlessness isn't a theory or a philosophical precept. It is a living Truth that must be seen to be believed and the best way to see it is to look at your own experience.

Everyone has problems. They may be financial, or a conflict at work or home, or a physical illness. Even when things are going well and there is abundance, problems still arise. Such daily problems come and go, simply a part of every human life. Those of us involved with the Twelve Steps are concerned with a different kind of problem. Be it alcohol, drugs, food, gambling, obsessive spiritual seeking, sex or what is loosely described as co-dependency, an addiction doesn't come and go. Unlike passing problems, addictions take root and then grow relentlessly, invading and poisoning every aspect of life. They eventually become indistinguishable from the life itself. Instead of having a problem, we ARE the problem! It seems that if we destroy the problem, we will destroy ourselves.

Most people come to the Twelve Steps because they have an addiction to something. An addict, in a moment of clarity, may catch a glimpse of his or her own powerlessness in relation to a particular substance or behavior. Usually in the beginning, it is simply that, a glimpse. To simply say "I have a problem with something" is an important start. It is the beginning of recognition of our own powerlessness.

Prior to coming to the Steps, my life revolved around trying to get MORE power. It seemed to me that all my problems resulted from not having enough power. I couldn't imagine how admitting powerlessness could help me. Little did I expect when I first cracked open the Big Book of AA that it would be the doorway into a life unimaginable. All I really knew in that moment was that something big and probably tragic happened to me the night before. I was uncomfortably sober and feeling very much alone in what I assumed was a unique situation. Though my view of the future was bleak and pessimistic, the Big Book was an immediate revelation. I was revolted by the relentless mentioning of God, yet I identified immediately with the behaviors and feelings described. There was something there calling to me, but I didn't know what it was. Today, I can look back and see that I was like a child playing with diamonds. I was attracted by the shiny brightness, but I had no idea of the enormous value of what I held in my hands.

The people in that first 7AM meeting didn't seem at all like me. After all, I had been up for the better part of four days, the booze was oozing out of my pores and my attitude towards life was anything but positive. The other people in the meeting were not like that. It seemed improbable that I might gain anything by associating with them. Had I the power to control things, I would have gladly returned to the life I lived for so many years and I would, unquestionably, now be long dead. But that power to control things was not mine and though it would be a while before I realized it, it had *never* been mine.

From my current perspective as a teacher of The Living Teaching of Advaita, I see that if one could completely and absolutely get the First Step's message of powerlessness (with all of its implications), there would be no need for the next eleven Steps. But that is a huge "if." During all the years of my association with the Steps, I have never met anyone who saw it all immediately. For most of us, it is a gradual process.

THE FALSE SENSE OF AUTHORSHIP

The question of personal power is central to both Step One and the Living Teaching. To better address this question, I use the term "False Sense of Authorship," or FSA for short. As it is quite important, and sometimes difficult to recognize, we will examine this False Sense of Authorship in detail throughout this book.

For the first years of our lives, we human beings exist in a state of wonder and immediate Presence, alternating between contentment and discomfort, happiness and sadness, pleasure and pain. Then at about the age of two years old, something happens within us. It is something that happens to every human being. We begin to view the world differently. We begin to labor under the sense that we are separate, independent and powerful. It is, in fact, one of the most common human beliefs. Our parents, schools, churches and society constantly reinforce this sense that we are separate and powerful. Symbolic of this, we cease referring to ourselves in the third person and begin referring to ourselves as "I."

From this turning point, we begin to amass a catalogue of things that "I" can do. We learn the names of things and develop the ability to perform tasks without the aid of our parents. The sense that not only can we *do* them, but we also *authored* them, accompanies nearly every one of these things. To "author" something means feeling that "I" am the independent and exclusive source of its creation. When we claim authorship, we say, " 'I' generate the power to make things happen and to control things." There is only one problem. This sense, though universally believed to be true, upon further investigation actually proves to be false. Investigation is essential. Recognizing that we have this False Sense of Authorship (FSA) and then recognizing that it is indeed false, is the key to realizing something unexpected and quite extraordinary. But in order to see, we first have to look.

For those of you who are familiar with the Big Book, perhaps it will be helpful to think of the FSA as what the Big Book calls the "self" or the "ego." For now, there is no need to delve too deeply into this sense of power we call the FSA, but it is useful to see if you can identify that it exists within you. Pause here for a minute and simply take a look into yourself. **See if you can recognize that within you is a sense that you make things happen, a sense that you author things.** Can you identify within yourself a sense of responsibility for making sure things turn out well? Do you ever feel guilty when things go badly? If so, it is tied to the sense that you have the power to author things.

I urge you not to skip this. Please put the book down and take a moment to consider....

~ ~ ~

If you blew right through without bothering to pause, I can identify. I probably would have done the same thing. All is not lost. We will continue to look at this sense as we progress and perhaps you will see it as we go forward. While it is a crucially important part of this book and the key to the understanding that this book hopes to foster, there is no need to figure it all out immediately. For now it is enough to merely cast a glance inward, to perhaps catch a glimpse of the sense of power and control that resides there.

ARE WE POWERLESS?

The Steps and the Living Teaching must have a point of entry to have an impact. For me, once the fog of drugs and alcohol lifted, it was plain to see that during the previous nineteen years, those substances controlled me. I hadn't controlled them. Or to put it in the terms of the Steps, I was powerless over alcohol. Each person has their own moment of clarity in which the Truth of how things actually ARE is glimpsed. How, or when this comes, is impossible to predict.

Once this moment of clarity occurs, we face the naked truth that if we did have power over the substance or behavior that first brought us to the Steps, we would have stopped it as soon as we noticed it created problems for us. We are forced to conclude that either we didn't have the power to see it, or we didn't have the power to stop it. This is the entry point into the recognition of personal powerlessness.

Unfortunately, the question of powerlessness is rarely simple. It is complicated by the fact that from time to time we have the *appearance* of control. We have the thought "I don't think I'll engage in my addictive behavior today" and then we don't engage in it. This correlation between our intention and a successful outcome fuels the False Sense of Authorship (FSA) and its claim of power to control things. The fact that on a hundred other occasions we had the same intention, but acted contrary to our intent, isn't even considered by the FSA. The Big Book says that the great obsession of every alcoholic is to "control and enjoy his drinking."[5] Another way of saying this is that an alcoholic desires to have power over alcohol.

In considering your personal power or powerlessness, you may want to look into these questions: If you can control something one time out of ten, does that mean you have power over it? How about if you can control it half of the time? Do you then have power over it? How about if you can control it the majority of the time? Or, is power an all or nothing proposition? Do you, or do you not have power over something?

The First Step revolves around these questions. No one can answer them for you. As long as you believe you have some kind of power (even partial or occasional power) over your problem substance or behavior, there is no point in proceeding further in the Steps. Hopefully, at some point you will see that it really is an all or nothing proposition. To say you sometimes have power over something and at other times not, is saying ultimately you are not in control. Do you know when your apparent power will work and when it won't? If you could control it, wouldn't it work all the time? Can you see that though you sometimes have the *appearance* of power, *you still don't have the ability to control when you have it and when you don't?* This is the recognition of ultimate powerlessness that the First Step points to.

A beautiful aspect of the Steps is that they do not try to convince you of anything. They aren't rules or gospel truths... they are guides. Thus, the Steps don't tell you that you are powerless, they invite you to examine the question for yourself. You are free to draw your own conclusions, though the Steps remain steadily there to challenge your conclusions should you delude yourself.

If you can have a glass or two of wine with your meals and still live a productive life, by all means do so. If you are a spiritual seeker and you can integrate your spiritual pursuits into a rich and fulfilling life, no problem. If you can go to the racetrack every now and then and bet whatever you can afford to lose, enjoy yourself! If you can have a single scoop of ice cream and then put the container back in the fridge until the next day — no problem — "our hats are off"[6] to you as they say in the Big Book. But if you can't, then perhaps you have reached the doorway to recognizing your own powerlessness, at least over this one thing.

The people who wrote the Steps introduce them by saying, "Here are the Steps we took which are suggested as a program of recovery."[7] They don't tell you what you should do or what you should believe. Rather, they share their "experience, strength and hope,"[8] inviting you to take from it whatever you find valuable.

I suppose this is as good a place as any to point out that there is no centralized authority in any of the Twelve Step programs. The only requirement for membership is a desire to stop the behavior that brings you to the Steps in the first place. In practical terms, this means that there is incredible diversity in the interpretation and practice of the Steps. People being people, organize themselves into groups and subgroups, each with strongly held opinions and convictions about the best way to do things. The ongoing miracle of the Twelve Steps and the various associated programs is that they are elastic enough to contain all of these emotions, fervent beliefs, volatile personalities and opinions without breaking.

UNMANAGEABILITY

The second part of the First Step says that the people who wrote the Steps discovered through their own self-examination that not only were they powerless over alcohol, but that their lives were unmanageable. This ups the ante on the question of powerlessness. You might acknowledge that you can't control the thing that brought you to the Steps, but not being able to manage your life is another matter. This is particularly the case if you still have a job, a home, a family, etc. The FSA will claim credit for these saying, "Look how well I am managing. If it weren't for me (the FSA), you wouldn't have any of these things. It was me who made you get out of bed to go to work and it was me who gave you the ability to sustain a relationship. I am responsible for it. And don't you forget it!" It is a voice both loud and familiar — after all, it has been with you since you were two years old. The question we look at throughout this book is: Is what that voice says true?

It is reminiscent of a scene I saw in Mumbai, India on a busy road up to Malabar Hill. We drove past a man sitting at ground level on a pallet of rough boards right next to the stunning chaos of Indian city traffic. As the tires of cars, trucks and buses whistled by within inches of him, he sat calmly swinging his arm, directing the flow of wildly honking drivers down the road past him. He was the "poster boy" for what we are calling the FSA – that aspect of ourselves that claims (falsely) to be in control.

Were you to ask this man by the side of the road what might happen if he stopped directing the traffic, he would undoubtedly paint a grim picture of accidents, traffic jams and irresponsible driving. He might then point with pride at how well things move with him in charge.

I can only imagine his response if you had the temerity to mention that while it was true that traffic flowed smoothly at that moment, there were several accidents and traffic jams earlier that day! The industrious fellow would undoubtedly concede that occasionally there were problems, but I'm sure he believed that without him sitting there swinging his arm, they would have been MUCH WORSE!

MEETING RAMESH S. BALSEKAR

Two years after being "struck sober," I had the very good fortune to meet a most extraordinary man. His name was Ramesh S. Balsekar and he was in my hometown of Los Angeles speaking to small groups of interested people about nondualism and powerlessness through a little known (outside of India) teaching called Advaita. As gurus from India go, he was quite unusual. He was the recently retired President of the Bank of India, educated at the London School of Economics; a family man, an avid golfer, very much a "man of this world." He didn't set himself apart. He didn't wear robes, live in an ashram or mouth flowery platitudes about what you should and should not do. In a most down-to-earth way, he spoke about discovering for yourself what was "Real" and what was false. He encouraged people to question their long held truths in the hope that they might see beyond the limited appearance, to the Infinite, of which the limited is made.

Not long after meeting him, I had occasion to share with him my feelings of insecurity about my lack of "spiritual" background. I had already told him about my recent recovery from active alcoholism and the subsequent pursuit of answers about this Higher Power that led me to meet him. But most of the people who came to his meetings were veteran spiritual seekers and I was an admitted novice, barely two years out of the bars and drug houses. So I often felt as lost and out of place as a kindergartener in a calculus class. With characteristic patience and kindness, he acquainted me with the concept of *sadhana*. *Sadhana* is a Sanskrit word meaning "the path to accomplishing something." Usually, it is associated with such traditional practices as meditation, chanting, devotion, being of service to others and prayer. He told me that *sadhana* described the means by which there sometimes comes a crack in the armor of the False Sense of Authorship. He said, "In your case, Wayne, the *sadhana* was to drink and take drugs for all those years!"

I can't, in good conscience, recommend to anyone that they try to follow my particular *sadhana* with the expectation that they will have the same results I had. This type of *sadhana* is too likely to kill you. But over the years I have met many people whose *sadhana* was some sort of addictive behavior. The major difference is that most people engaged in traditional *sadhana* believe they are responsible for doing it, whereas for those with *sadhana* of addiction, there is almost universal recognition that they are not in control of at least, their addiction. When there is recovery it is often seen that it was simply a happening that ultimately turned out well — Grace.

As a teacher of Advaita, most of the people I meet with are not addicts in the traditional sense (though many have had what could be termed as an addiction to spiritual seeking). I have observed that people with addictions are propelled into the possibility of powerlessness in a different way than non-addicts.

Most non-addicts that come to hear me talk about the Living Teaching, have had some kind of dramatic and often traumatic life event. This type of event triggers a moment of clarity in which they glimpse the underlying Unity of all things. A desire to understand, or to "return" to this Unity often provokes spiritual seeking. Some have spontaneously felt or even recognized their own personal powerlessness in some way. The Living Teaching serves as an entry point to further explore these initial insights. What provides the initial opening to the possibility of personal powerlessness is not important. It is the opening itself that is crucial. Without it, the notion of being personally powerless remains for most people a ridiculous, perhaps even dangerous, idea.

The Living Teaching is nothing more than a collection of pointers aimed at identifying the False Sense of Authorship — that sense all human beings get at around two years old that they are separate, independent and powerful entities. The Living Teaching also encourages a deep inquiry into this sense to determine if it is actually true. The reason for this focus is that the *sense* that I am separate, independent and powerful (the FSA) is connected to all suffering in life. We feel guilty because we have the *sense* that we could have and should have acted differently. We hate others because we have the *sense* that they could have and should have acted better towards us, or that they deliberately chose to harm us. Opening to the possibility that there is another way to look at things is a great blessing indeed! The benefits of such openness are not esoteric or abstract. Seeing the Truth of What Is in this moment relieves us of the bondage of the FSA, allowing us to walk the earth peacefully regardless of circumstances.

> Once in a while it really hits people that they don't have to experience the world in the way they have been told to.
> –Alan Keightley

The Living Teaching encourages you to look carefully into your own experiences, particularly those experiences infused with guilt and pride. With Grace, you will identify the ultimate Source of your thoughts, feelings and actions, indeed of your very existence.

As I said earlier, no one I have ever met has taken Step One totally and completely, with all its implications, the first time through. At this early point in the Steps, we are not expected to believe anything other than that we are powerless over the one thing bringing us so low that we need help, and that our lives could use some improvement. The journey from recognizing that *some* things are out of our control, to *knowing* intuitively that *everything* is out of our control, may be long. But the Steps are patient — far more patient than we are.

The next eleven Steps comprise a magnificent blueprint for turning this initial opening into an enduring reality.

May it find you now.

STEP TWO

"Came to believe that a
Power greater than ourselves
could restore us to sanity."

The people who wrote the Steps state that their purpose is to "enable you to find a Power greater than yourself which will solve your problem."[9] Notice that they said the power greater than you "will solve your problem." They did NOT say that this power would help YOU to solve your problem. It is an important distinction. In Step One, you admitted you were powerless over something and that to some degree you could not manage your own life. Simply put, Step One is about recognizing that you have a problem you can't fix with your own power. This may or may not be news to you.

In Step Two, we catch our first glimpse of a solution that doesn't depend on us. This is often a big hurdle. The FSA is strong in its claim of running the show and while it may have been dealt a bit of a blow in Step One, it is resilient. The FSA is very likely to admit at this point that it could maybe use a little help with solving the problem and may propose a partnership of sorts with God. God can be the silent partner in the enterprise. God can supply a little power and we (the FSA) will manage and control the rest. Much of the world's population operates on this model. But both Advaita and the Steps are pointing to a radical possibility, something far bigger and more complete.

If you look deeply into your experience of your own sense of power, you may recognize that the FSA will seize every opportunity to reassert itself. If there is recovery for the addict in a Twelve Step program, the FSA will be quick to claim the credit, pointing to the good program it has worked and the willpower it has exerted. If there is relapse, the FSA will claim credit in the form of blame for missing meetings, not trying hard enough or simply being bad. For the spiritual seeker, if there is progress in reducing the sense of personal power and control, the FSA will point with pride at this spiritual advancement. If the sense of personal power and control reasserts itself, the FSA will claim that it must redouble its efforts to return to higher consciousness!

The FSA is simply another name for that quality within us that "plays God." It claims to be the author and thus responsible for our thoughts, feelings and actions. Even more insidious than that, it claims to actually BE us. This has been going on for so long that there is no longer any doubt. We simply assume we are the authors of our thoughts, feelings and actions. The critical question raised directly in the Living Teaching and indirectly through the Steps is: Are these claims true?

INSANITY

There is a phrase in Step Two you probably noticed— "restore us to sanity." To be restored to sanity implies we are currently insane — a proposition many of us think is a little harsh. If you have a problem with this, it may be useful to define the term. Insanity need not be restricted to a picture of a locked ward and restraints. One popular definition of insanity is to keep on repeating the same behavior while expecting different results. This definition enables anyone qualifying for any Twelve Step program to see that insanity within his or her own self. "I'll just have one drink. I'll just eat one cookie. I'll just make one bet. I'll bail him out one last time. This time it will be different. This time I will be in control. This time it won't lead to any problems." Could we be any crazier?

Within the Living Teaching of Advaita, the definition of insanity is to live a delusional existence; to be out of step with the way things actually are. This definition is both subtle and challenging. How can we know if our perceptions are delusional, particularly if most of the people around us share the same delusion? In the Living Teaching, the proposed solution is to look deeply within ourselves with curiosity and an open mind, learning all the while that it is a Power Greater Than Ourselves (God, Source, Consciousness) that fuels the looking.

I suppose I should stop here and talk a bit about my initial attitude towards the concept of God. When I first looked at the Steps, I had an arrogant and ultimately unexamined antipathy to the very idea of God. It was a prejudice, though at the time I'm sure I would have told you it was a logical and well-considered conclusion. As far as I was concerned, God was a man-made concept invented to explain the unexplainable, a superstition. Believing in God was a sign of personal weakness. Furthermore, it was a concept that had been used for unspeakable evils, from the Crusades to the Inquisition, to uncountable *jihads* and holy wars, not to mention the depraved, predatory and often drunken priests continuously in the headlines. To debunk religion and by extension, God, was as easy as shooting fish in a barrel — and it still is.

Profoundly wise, the Steps didn't try to convince me I was wrong. Then and now, they stay unconnected to any organized religion or definition of what God is or isn't. In terms of doctrine, there simply isn't anything to disagree with, ridicule or debunk. Without the distraction of an assertion to debate, I was left to look into myself. A space was created in which I began asking some very fundamental and ultimately liberating questions.

What I found most challenging was trying to figure out the Truth behind all the concepts. To be literally struck sober in the middle of the night, without warning and without any desire to be sober, left me in an awkward position. My long held atheistic belief that I was the master of my own destiny was shaken at the root. There was no question that the obsession that lived within me for so long was gone. It was equally clear to me that I hadn't made it go away. So what had?

For those having difficulty with the concept of God or Higher Power I would like to offer another way of looking at it: Circumstance. When you look at your own history you can easily see how Circumstance entered into your life and propelled you in new directions. A stranger walks in the door, you meet and your life changes. You fall in love, or you are introduced to a new way of looking at things and suddenly your world is different. This is the power of Circumstance and the most significant quality of Circumstance is that you are powerless to control it.

An exercise in the Living Teaching is to take a long piece of paper, turn it horizontally and then draw a line horizontally across the center. This is the timeline of your life. At the start of the line write the word "birth" and then begin to chronologically record the significant events of your life. If you consider them positive write them above the line (the more positive you consider them, the higher above the line you write them). If you consider the event negative write it below the line (the worse you consider it, the further below you write it). Do this for all the significant events right up to the present moment. When you are done, look to see the role of Circumstance in these life events. It will be a revelation.

The Steps are a journey, not a destination. Step Two is, for some of us, a mini-journey all its own. Coming to believe that there is a power greater than our egoic self that is responsible for everything is a gradual process. Looking back on it, now many years later, I see that it crept up on me while I was busy trying to creep up on it. But at the beginning I was on a mission. I wanted answers and with typical impatience, I wanted them Now!

I mentioned that recognizing powerlessness over at least one thing in Step One is like a crack in the wall. After completing Step One, the crack in the wall of delusion that the FSA spent most of my life building widened a bit. It was still small, but it did allow enough light to shine through for me to realize it was there. Once I saw that light, I began digging out through the crack, widening it a little at a time. This digging took several forms.

Of the many blessings I received, one of the greatest was meeting Lee. Lee was nine years sober and recently returned from a spiritual pilgrimage to India. He had accumulated a large and diverse spiritual library in which he invited me to graze. He told me, "Take whatever attracts you, try it and if isn't to your taste, bring it back and try something else."

In this way I was exposed to the writings of Christian mystics such as Joel Goldsmith and Meister Eckhart, Buddhists such as Thich Nhat Han and Pema Chodron, Taoist writers Lao Tzu and Chuang Tzu, modern Hindus such as Osho and Ram Dass, plus an assortment of mystic Jews, Sufis and eclectics like Alan Watts.

These were all vastly different perspectives from diverse cultures stretching over thousands of years, and yet they all seemed to point toward a singular Truth. I couldn't grasp exactly what that Truth was, but I knew in my guts that it was there.

I read in the Big Book, "We found that as soon as we lay aside prejudice and expressed even a willingness to believe in a power greater than ourselves, we commenced to get results, even though it was impossible for any of us to fully define or comprehend that Power, which is God." [10]

I'm not sure I can truthfully say that I expressed a willingness to believe in a power greater than myself, but the certainty that there must be something bigger than my egoic self (FSA) continued growing. The assertion that "it is impossible for any of us to fully define or comprehend that Power..."[11] left the door wide open. I was even willing to forgive them for continuing to call that indefinable Power God, and speaking about it as a Him. I slowly began to let go of the suspicion that this was all part of an elaborate hidden scheme to get me to believe in the apparently masculine humanoid God of *their* understanding.

For those who come to the Steps with strongly held religious or spiritual convictions, Step Two provides a more subtle challenge. Can you look at what you believe with fresh eyes and an open mind? Step Two is a call to reaffirm what you believe by examining it in the light of contemplation and openness. People who go through this process often report a strengthening of faith and an enlivening of their beliefs.

The Living Teaching's perspective on this Step is that we are all insane from the age of two years old. From birth to age two, we live in perfect harmony with life as it is. We like what we like; we dislike what we don't like. We react in the moment to what is happening in accordance with the temperament with which we were born (genetics), modified by our experiences since birth (conditioning). All of our thoughts, feelings and actions are spontaneous and immediate. Then, sometime around the age of two, it is as if a switch is flipped inside of us. We begin to live a delusional existence. We start to see ourselves as separate, independent entities. We begin to believe ourselves capable of authoring our own thoughts, feeling and actions.

It is a dramatic, life altering change. We suddenly go from having "wants" to having "shoulds." Our desires are no longer simple and direct; they become complicated by the notion that we "should" be able to get what we want.

After all, aren't we independent and powerful? We "should" be able to make that which we desire happen.

When this change happens we begin to suffer for the first time, a period sometimes called The Terrible Twos. As babies, we certainly felt pain and frustration, but now the pain and frustration is amplified a hundredfold by the sense that IT SHOULDN'T BE THIS WAY!

In the Living Teaching, we make an important distinction between pain and suffering. Pain is a reaction that occurs in the moment. Suffering is the projection of the pain out of the reality of the moment into the fantasy world of the past and the future. The story of what "should have been" and what "will probably be next" is the amplifier converting pain into suffering. Pain comes from not liking what is happening. Suffering comes from feeling that what is happening *should* not be happening.

Liking and not liking, and the pleasure and pain that naturally follow, is a functional part of being human. When someone close to us dies, we experience pain in the moment from the sense of loss that arises from the absence of the beloved. If we feel that the person close to us should not have died, that we or someone else was responsible or could have prevented the death, then the pain of the loss turns into suffering. It is when dislike becomes "should not be" that we suddenly find ourselves in conflict with the entire Universe and we suffer. Simply put, suffering results from the story the FSA weaves around the pain that exists in the moment.

Most of us develop mechanisms to cope with this suffering. Without some kind of relief valve, we would be unable to live in our families and societies. These mecha-

nisms often take the forms of elaborate fantasies support-
ing the notion of our independent power and ability to
control. We believe these fantasies to be true despite an
abundance of evidence to the contrary. The fact that nearly
everyone around us shares similar fantasies makes it no
less crazy.

Both the Steps and the Living Teaching are attempts to
restore us to the sanity we knew before the age of two
years old. By recognizing our fundamental powerlessness
as separate individuals we do not suddenly become help-
less babies again, rather we reawaken to the reality that
lies before us and we begin to live in sane harmony with
what is actually happening. Such harmonious living,
though sometimes painful, is free of suffering.

THE OCEAN AND THE WAVE

The Living Teaching's perspective on Step Two is that
the reason a power greater than ourselves must be responsible for breaking the delusion, and thus restoring us to
sanity, is because it is this same Power which is ultimately
responsible for doing absolutely EVERYTHING.

A metaphor commonly used in The Living Teaching is
that of the Ocean and the wave. I will refer to it again and
again throughout this book, so please take a moment to
consider it. In this metaphor all there is, is Ocean. It is all
that exists. The term Ocean points to the same Essence as
the terms God, Source, Consciousness, Unity etc., but the
image of Ocean is familiar and useful. When the Ocean
goes into movement (Big Bang/Genesis) it forms waves.
The waves are the "things" that exist, forming the mani-

fest Universe. Waves are temporary as are all things, be they galaxies, humans or atoms. They have a beginning, duration and an end. Waves also have qualities that we can compare and catalogue. As human beings, we are waves. We have various qualities that constantly change and we have a beginning, duration, and an end. It is crucial to recognize that a wave is a movement of energy in the ocean. A wave is not a separate packet of water moving through the ocean. When we stand on the shore and watch a wave approach, the water of the wave is not moving toward us. The wave is actually the expression of the energy moving *through* the water.

Human waves possess one quality that differentiates us from all other types of waves. As discussed earlier, we human waves develop a peculiar sense around age two. We have the sense that we are not waves but that we are separate and independent droplets. As separate, independent entities, we can then claim to have independent power. The sense that we are separate, independent and powerful entities is what we refer to when we use the term "False Sense of Authorship (FSA)."

Remember, we began by saying that the Ocean is all that exists. This means in reality there is no place outside the Ocean in which a droplet *could* exist. Therefore the sense of separation and independence must be, by definition, a false sense. It is nonsensical to say there is Everything PLUS me. Yet nonsensical or not, it is a sense shared by virtually all human beings after the age of two. So our common, collective human experience is an agreed upon assertion of independent, personal power. But just because nearly everyone agrees that this is true does not necessarily make it true.

Both The Living Teaching and the Twelve Steps aim to foster a spiritual awakening in which there is direct recognition of oneself as a wave (not a separate droplet), and by extension, knowing oneself as Ocean. Once this is clearly seen, the sense of separation and the false claim of independent personal power (FSA) evaporate. What remains is Peace that surpasses all understanding. This is the restoration to sanity talked about in the Step Two.

May it find you now.

STEP THREE

"Made a decision to turn our will and our lives
over to the care of God as we understood Him."

There are five frogs sitting on a log.
Three of them make the decision to jump off.
How many are left?

The answer is: Five.
Three decided to jump, but none of them actually did it.

If you look at your life, as you will hopefully do in Step Four, you will see that you made many decisions that never actualized. Yet, unconsciously, we have come to associate a decision with an action in a cause and effect relationship. We say that the decision *caused* the action. But is that strictly true? If it were true, wouldn't every decision lead inevitably to its linked action? Since our own life experience shows us that it doesn't, there must be at least one other factor involved. Both the Steps and the Living Teaching are concerned with helping you discover the exact nature of the other factor(s).

Hint: the Steps use the terms God and power greater than yourself. The Living Teaching of Advaita uses the terms Source, Higher Power, Circumstance, Consciousness and Ocean.

As all of us know only too well, it is far easier to decide to do something than to actually do it. (Could it be because we are powerless?) So the creators of the Steps give us a break here. In this Step, they only invite us to *decide* to turn our will and our lives over to this power they call God. From the perspective of the Living Teaching, this is absolutely brilliant since your will and your life are understood to ALREADY be in the care of God... and always have been. The decision is merely another step in realizing the condition that actually exists. But since the FSA probably remains strong and active at this stage, the Steps throw it a bone to keep it busy. It is as if the Steps are saying, "Go ahead and claim responsibility for your decisions since it may be a while before the False Sense of Authorship is removed. Besides, the work is about to start with Step Four and you will be so busy taking stock of things, you probably won't even notice."

PROBLEMS

Everyone has problems. Be they money problems, relationship problems, health problems, sex problems, emotional problems or even problems resulting from abundance in life, there is no escaping them. Even if you are relieved of the problem that brought you initially to the Steps, even if you surrender completely to God and are freed from the bondage of self, you will continue to experience life situations we can group under the umbrella titled "problems." The questions frequently arising at this point are, "What do I do about my problems if I am powerless? How do I live? How can I manage?"

The Big Book says that we must "be convinced that any life run on self-will can hardly be a success."[12] This is a pretty strong statement considering that nearly everyone you talk to thinks that strong willpower is the necessary component in success. This statement thus seems to fly in the face of popular wisdom. Once again, the Steps suggest a vision of a life previously unimagined. They propel us towards the insight that our lives are run by a power greater than ourselves rather than by our own self-will. What is truly extraordinary about this is that as this vision grows, we find ourselves aligned with how things actually are. We begin to suffer less. Our problems become simply problems that inevitably come and go. We worry less and find we have far more energy to deal with the problem at hand. By almost any definition this would be called "success." This vision is the same as the one pointed to by the Living Teaching of Advaita.

"WE HAD TO QUIT PLAYING GOD."[13]

Step Two was the simple recognition that we COULD be restored to sanity. It is extremely rare that we actually ARE restored to sanity at this point. So the Steps meet us right where we are — still believing we have at least some personal power that we can manage with self-will. Step Three turns the notion of self-will back on itself. It says, OK if you have the power to do things, try surrendering, try turning your self-will over to this Higher Power. Try to quit playing God. If you try and fail, don't be discouraged. The founders of AA who made every effort to surrender realized that, "there often seems no way of entirely getting rid of self without His (God's) aid."[14] This makes complete sense when you recognize your own powerlessness. What may on the surface seem like your authored "doing" reveals itself as the product of an entirely different Source altogether.

> "As we felt new power flow in, as we enjoyed peace of mind, as we discovered we could face life successfully, as we became conscious of His presence, we began to lose our fear of today, tomorrow or the hereafter. We were reborn."[15]

These lines from the Big Book points out one of the many seeming paradoxes found throughout the process of spiritual awakening. As we recognize our own personal powerlessness, as we surrender to a Power Greater Than Ourselves, we begin to feel "new power flow in." This new power has a very different quality than the power claimed by the FSA. This power flows through us, but does not originate with us. Such power enlightens us while the power claimed by the FSA serves only to weigh us down with responsibilities and obligations we cannot possibly fulfill, dooming us always to ultimate failure.

This decision we make in Step Three to surrender the idea of self-will is critical to successfully taking the next step. You must take a power greater than yourself into Step Four. Your interior landscape is like a bad neighborhood in which you don't want to go alone. If you still firmly believe that self-will is the superior approach to life, you are bound to flounder in Step Four.

With Grace, it may be possible to move forward in this process of surrendering to What Is. It is most often a realization that gradually deepens. The purpose of the Steps that follow, often called the "Action Steps," is to facilitate this deepening.

Readers who have had no addiction to a substance or behavior such as drugs, gambling or spiritual seeking, but have had an opening to the possibility of their own powerlessness, may also find benefit in the Steps that follow. There is still much, much more to discover.

May it find you now.

STEP FOUR

"Made a searching and fearless
moral inventory of ourselves."

The very essence of life is to be discovered in our relationships. Relationships to people and events often define who we are. As we catalog these relationships, we may begin to see patterns emerge. Although these patterns defined us in the past, they need not bind us in the future.

How you relate to other people, how you relate to events that happen, how you relate to your own thoughts and actions and how you relate to a power greater than your imagined separate self, are the building blocks of your life. To understand yourself you must first take stock of these relationships. Selfishness, dishonesty, resentment and fear are the things that keep us from having successful relationships and so ultimately, a successful life. In Step Four we look at them and put down on paper how they manifested in our lives up to this point.

OUR STORY

In Step Four and again in Step Twelve, we tell our story. Everybody has a story. Our lives are our story. The more genuine, authentic and honest we are as a storyteller, the more successful we will be with Steps Four and Twelve. Tell the truth — that is our motto. As we gain humility we begin to acknowledge that our truth, the story we tell of our life, is not true in an objective, absolute way. None of us has a monopoly on the truth. Our beliefs and the filter of memory color it. We know that others often see things far differently. Our perspective is liable to change and when it does, our own truth may change. That said, our truth of the moment is all we have to work with and you are encouraged to use it to the best of your ability while remaining open to the fact that more may be revealed in the future.

HOW TO DO STEP FOUR

Perhaps the most beautiful aspect of the Steps is that they are alive and flexible. Just as AA's founders modified the very Christian Steps of The Oxford Group to suit the needs of a diverse band of recovering alcoholics, AA's Twelve Steps have been adapted to help people recover from a wide range of debilitating conditions. Like bamboo, the Steps have been bent to many purposes without breaking.

In addition to the original instructions found in chapter five of the Big Book, there are literally hundreds, if not thousands, of detailed guides to working Step Four. Step Four is one of those things in life that is impossible to do wrong. The most important thing is to do it.

Some people write Step Four as an autobiography, recording everything they remember about their lives. While this is certainly one approach, unless you are a very fast writer this can be enormously time consuming and runs the risk of boring to death the person you share this all with in Step Five. The approach found in the Big Book is far more focused and streamlined, not to mention quite a bit easier. It suggests making lists of significant events in our lives, using four columns consisting of WHO, WHAT HAPPENED, HOW IT AFFECTED ME, WHAT IS MY PART IN THIS? The areas of particular emphasis are resentments, fears, sex and guilt.

Before you begin, this may feel like an overwhelming and impossible task. Large-scale projects frequently seem impossible when viewed from outside. I would compare it to writing a book. Every time I begin a new book project I hear a loud voice that says I can't write a book. I am too lazy. I hate to write. I have nothing anybody wants to hear. It has all been said before. Etc. Yet, most days I can write a sentence. Sometimes after I write a sentence, I end up writing a paragraph. On a good day, I write several paragraphs that add up to a page or two. After six months or a year or five years, all of these sentences and paragraphs and pages add up to a book. In fact, this is my fifth book in twenty years, but each time I sit down to do it I have the feeling I'll never be able to write a book. It is simply too big a task!

Writing a Fourth Step inventory is the same. There is no need to try to do the whole thing at once. Do as much as you can and no more. Try to do a little each day. Be gentle with yourself, if you can. Relaxing and taking it easy is not necessarily the same as being lazy.

If you have access to someone who has been through the entire Twelve Step process and appears to have benefited from it, I would encourage you to ask him or her for help. They may be able to warn you of pitfalls in the process as well as offer the strength of their own experience.

Step Four speaks of a moral inventory. I must admit that my first reaction to this was suspicious concern that the Steps were trying to get me in line with their Judeo-Christian morality. Once I calmed down and looked deeper into it, I realized that "moral" simply means "right and wrong." The infinitely spacious Steps allow room for our own definition of right and wrong. We are not expected to adopt any particular group's definition. I realized that in taking a moral inventory, I was to write down the things that I had done that *I* considered to be right and wrong, good and bad in my life. In short, I was asked to be honest with and about myself, particularly in regards to my relationships with others.

While others are obviously necessary for a relationship to exist, the emphasis of Step Four is ourselves. It is suggested that we try not to take the inventory of the others — as tempting as that often is!

WHAT VERSUS WHY

When doing a personal inventory, it may be helpful to pay close attention to the difference between looking at the "what" of things versus looking at the "why" of things. "Why" is a story we tell about what actually happened. The story of "why" is a fantasy, distracting us from the "what" which is our experience. "What" is far more immediate and holistic, while "why" is always relative and subjective.

In Step Four, we try to keep our focus on the "what" of things, not the "why" of things. When we tell the "what" of things, we are in far less danger of being self-serving or critical. It is far, far easier to simply write down what we have done, what we are afraid of, what we are resentful about, what we feel guilty about, what we have done sexually, etc., than to try to figure out why. When looking at the causes and conditions of those incidents important enough to make our inventory list, we focus on *what* caused them, *what* conditions contributed to their very existence. This perspective ultimately takes us back to Source (the Ocean). We eventually come to realize that Source, (Ocean) disguised as events, (waves) was responsible.

You may find that your mind keeps trying to shift the focus away from the "what" and back to the "why." Just remember that the "why" is the realm where the FSA is king. It rules over all the could-haves and should-haves. Why didn't I do it this way? Why did I do it that way? "Why" leads to speculation and uncertainty. "What" grounds us in the truth of our own experience.

HONESTY

"Rarely have we seen a person fail who has thoroughly followed our path. Those who do not recover are people who cannot or will not completely give themselves to this simple program, usually men and women who are constitutionally incapable of being honest with themselves. There are such unfortunates. They are not at fault; they seem to have been born that way. They are naturally incapable of grasping and developing a manner of living which demands rigorous honesty. Their chances are less than average. There are those, too, who suffer from grave emotional and mental disorders, but many of them do recover if they have the capacity to be honest."[16]

This passage from the Big Book is read at the beginning of Twelve Step meetings throughout the world. Obviously, honesty is regarded as the key to success, but what is meant by the term honesty? We normally think of honesty in terms of conduct. If we don't steal, lie, or cheat, we are honest. Being honest with ourselves must therefore mean not to lie to ourselves or to cheat ourselves (a quality particularly important when doing Step Four).

Honesty within the Living Teaching has a markedly different meaning. Honesty becomes synonymous with recognizing the truth of What Is. This "What Is" includes absolutely everything — good and bad, beautiful and ugly. Wherever you look, there It is. Even the looking itself is It. Perhaps, you will discover that you (with all your faults and limitations) are It too.

> You must think small before you can think big.
> You must know yourself before you attempt to know God.
> Every journey is comprised of small steps.
> —Ram Tzu

GET IT DOWN ON PAPER

In Step Four, you write down on paper (or the modern technological equivalent) the qualities and features of that life you decided to turn over to a power greater than yourself in Step Three.

What is here, now? What am I like? What are my characteristics? (You are encouraged to be fearless and thorough in this). What is my sexual nature? What have people done to me and what have I done to others? What do I consider to be my assets? What are my liabilities? Do I have resentments? If so, what are they and do they all seem to have a common root? What role do I play in the continuation of these resentments?

Is there something you have done that up to that moment you swore you would never do? Perhaps it was something as simple as wagging your finger in the face of your child (an action your mother did that you promised you would never do to your own child). Or perhaps you had an extra-marital affair despite believing such behavior wrong. If you examine the history of your life you may recall several such "embarrassments." How is it that you did these things you were adamantly against?

The inventory process of Step Four offers a structure to work within when seeking answers to these questions. The Living Teaching of Advaita adds yet another layer of inquiry to the one proposed by the Steps.

Once you have a complete catalog of the ways in which you relate to others, to events and to yourself, the Living Teaching supports the effort of looking deeply into the question of what makes us behave the way we do. How is it that sometimes we are able to act in accordance with our values and at other times not? Where did these characteristics come from? What makes me the way I am? Did I make myself this way, or is the way I am the result of a vast complex of forces? Do I seem to see things differently from others? If so, is one of us right and the other wrong?

How can we be sure? What determines how I see things? What makes my vision of things change, sometimes dramatically? Who is doing all this? Who cares?!

The usual, surface claim of the FSA is that "I-the-FSA" was responsible. "I" could have and should have done better. "I" should have resisted the temptation. "I" should have been stronger, wiser. "I" should have been less self-centered, less selfish.

The Living Teaching encourages you to look ever deeper in order to see beyond the claim of the FSA. What were the causes and conditions preceding and surrounding the action itself? In the case of wagging your finger in your child's face, can you see how Universal forces contributed to your action? What were your hormone levels like at that moment? How about your blood sugar levels? What event had just occurred in your life that might have affected your mood? Was your sleep interrupted the night before? Did your other child just write all over the walls with pen? Did you just get news of an unexpected expense? Was there bad health news for you or a loved one? Can you recognize that there is no singular cause for anything?

What about the positive events in your life? Can you see that everything you have is a gift? Even if you think you worked hard and earned it. Can you see that your ability to earn it is a gift? You were given sufficient intelligence, drive, health and energy to do the earning. Consider this: Where does the power to earn come from?

Can you begin to see how each action is connected to a vast web of causes and conditions? Can you begin to see how your characteristics and behaviors are inextricably linked to genetics and life experiences (conditioning)?

When you see where your personal qualities actually come from, you will be less inclined to heed the voice of the FSA when it falsely claims responsibility for these qualities.

In looking, there may be seeing. In seeing, there may be Understanding.

> "Many of us had moral and philosophical convictions galore, but we could not live up to them even though we would have liked to. Neither could we reduce our self-centeredness much by wishing or trying on our own power."[17]

As we look at our resentments, fears and sexual history in Step Four, we may begin to see how our own moral and philosophical convictions sometimes diverge from our behavior. We believe, for example, it is right to be generous to others yet sometimes we act selfishly. We believe that we must be honest in our domestic relationship and yet we tell lies, big or small. In the Living Teaching, we delve into the ultimate Source of such behavior. Is it us? Or is it some power greater than us? Coming from a religious background, the creators of the Steps acknowledged that God had to "help" them to behave better. In the Living Teaching, the distinction between God and us blurs as our understanding deepens. But we get ahead of ourselves. Step Four is mainly about recording what is here and what has so far happened in our lives. Making sense of it comes later.

When the Steps discuss our negative behavior, they quickly suggest that we are not bad people, we are sick people. By suggesting we are sick, the Steps hope to keep us from getting mired in guilt. To say that we are sick is to introduce an outside influence to our actions. Many of us did horrible things both to ourselves and to others. As the inventory process brings these to the surface, the FSA claims responsibility, and guilt is a common and debilitating reaction. Sometimes it is so strong we feel we can't continue. When we are open to the possibility that we are sick rather than bad or evil, the guilt lessens and we are able to move forward again. Sickness is not an excuse for our actions. In Steps Eight and Nine we will see that we must still make amends for all these things we have done that hurt others.

Our inventory may also include some of the terrible things done to us by others (particularly as they are linked to our resentments). The main thing is to get it all down on paper, look at it and hopefully begin to see some of the patterns in this crazy life we've lived. When both our negative actions and the negative actions of others are seen as the product of a sickness over which none of us have control, the whole game changes. Resentment, guilt and hatred (both of ourselves and others) simply don't arise. It is miraculous.

The Big Book, with its religious perspective, advocates praying for the other's recovery from their sickness in much the same way that it advocates asking God to remove personal shortcomings. In the Living Teaching, this state of blamelessness and acceptance is the natural outcome of recognizing our absolute powerlessness through inquiring into who we truly are and intuitively seeing beyond the answer.

When taking a personal inventory it is easy to get distracted with questions of, "Am I being totally honest here? What if I'm not being honest enough? How can I even know if what I remember is true?" Many of us have found it is enough to simply say, "In this moment I am being as honest as I can." One of the tenants of the Twelve Step programs is that if you stick with it, a greater capacity for honesty is almost certain to develop as you move forward.

Step Four is not as complicated as people make it out to be. It is simply about looking at who and what you are. Start at the surface and work your way down. Look at yourself. Write down what you see. Consider it. It doesn't have to be a strenuous undertaking; try approaching it with simple curiosity, like a small child might watch an ant carrying a grain of sand in its jaws.

RESENTMENT

Making a list of resentments is one of the important tasks of Step Four. The Big Book says resentment is the "number one offender." It literally kills us by causing so much suffering that we seek relief or escape in our addictions.

> "Being convinced that self, manifested in various ways, was what had defeated us, we considered its common manifestations."[18]

What the Big Book calls "self," the Living Teaching calls the FSA. When making a list of resentments, you will likely find one word that keeps popping up over and over, "should." Our resentments are inevitably linked to what we believe others "should" have done or "should not" have done. This sense of "should" is insidious and deadly. It rots us from inside. It separates and isolates us.

If we look deeply into the matter, we may see that this "should" is a rejection of What Is. It is a claim by the FSA that "I" know how things *ought* to have happened. It is based in an arrogant belief that what I think is right and wrong is True in the absolute sense. This is different from likes and dislikes. Not liking what someone did and feeling that they *should* not have done it are actually two very different things. When I say I don't like something, essentially it reflects my preferences and the way I am created. I like some things and I don't like other things. When I say you "shouldn't" have done something, it is my judgment of you, based on a standard I believe to be unquestionably Right. Most importantly, I assume that you had the power in that moment not to do what you did. When I feel that you had the power not to do what I know to be unquestionably wrong, but you did it anyway, resentment inevitably follows.

Resentment is sometimes described as taking a dose of poison and hoping the other person will die. A temporary solution to this problem is forgiveness. But it is akin to cutting off the head of a weed. It almost inevitably grows back. A more permanent solution lies in digging out the resentment at the root and this involves Acceptance. Acceptance is the recognition that what happened could not have been otherwise and is no individual person's fault. Recognizing that my judgment about anything is relative, changeable and not Absolute, is implicit in Acceptance. Within Acceptance is the possibility that though I am convinced I am right, I might be wrong! This is also known as humility.

It is crucial to note that Acceptance is not the same as

approval. We can accept that something happened as a part of the functioning of the Universe, and still not like it. However, if a "should be otherwise" is present, then guilt or resentment will invariably follow.

The "should" applied to others leads to resentment. The "should" applied to oneself results in guilt and self-centered fear. The root of the "I should" is in the FSA's claim of power. When I say, "I should" have acted differently, there is an assumption that my action was a product of my personal power and I misused it. This is guilt. When I project what "I should" do into the future, some part of me knows that I lack sufficient power to control all the possible variables to insure success and the result is fear.

So once again, we are faced with the question of personal power. When we claim to have it, we inevitably suffer. When we are free of the inherently false claim of the FSA, our personal powerlessness is apparent and there is Peace. Such Peace is unconditional; it is there even when we are unhappy because we don't like something.

The Living Teaching seeks to foster the understanding that all of our actions and all of the actions of others are the product of a Higher Power as it plays out through the complexity of genetic predisposition combined with life experience (conditioning). We see this genetic predisposition in babies; some who are born passive while others are born active. As they grow, life experiences combine to either strengthen or modify the qualities they are born with and it is exactly the sum of these qualities in the moment that influences action. Therefore, all actions, both the good and bad, are not the product of independent personal power, as we previously thought. With such an understanding, we are no longer subject to guilt or pride for our actions, nor do we suffer the poisoning effects of hating others for their actions, no matter how much they hurt us.

The Big Book points to the fact that self (the FSA) manifests in a variety of ways. Because of this, we suffer. In Step Four we are encouraged to identify the various manifestations of the self (FSA) beginning first with resentments, then moving on to fears.

FEARS

"We reviewed our fears thoroughly. We put them on paper, even though we had no resentment in connection with them. We asked ourselves why we had them. Wasn't it because self-reliance failed us?"[19]

As with resentments, the connection between fear and self (FSA) is a crucial one. Step Four is designed to illuminate it. Most of us are taught from a very early age that self-reliance is a desirable and admirable quality and are encouraged to develop it. But to actually be self-reliant, we must call on personal power. Even if we consider ourselves independent, we know from our own life experience that personal power is limited. Fear arises when we recognize that we may not have sufficient power to do that which we feel we "should" do.

Once you have a list of fears it may become possible to see the common thread running through them. It always comes back to a feeling of insufficient power and lack of control.

The activity of the FSA makes us feel temporarily powerful and independent. It makes us believe we have the ability to control events and ourselves. With this supposed independence comes a feeling of isolation. Addiction amplifies that feeling. When addiction is active, we are left with the sense that we "should" be powerful as we constantly face the miserable evidence that we are weak. Those of us who are non-addicts also face evidence of what we consider to be weakness when we sometimes fail to act in accordance with our own moral and philosophical standards.

Within the context of the Living Teaching, weakness and powerlessness are two entirely different things. Weakness means that there is the *possibility* of personal power, but that we lack a sufficient amount of it. Powerlessness is the recognition that personal power is an illusion and that we have *never* had personal power, even when we thought we did. It is the great paradox of life that with the claim of personal power comes fear and weakness and with the recognition of our personal powerlessness comes genuine strength.

> "The spiritual life is not a theory.
> We have to live it."[20]

Powerlessness is not helplessness, nor is it fatalism. When we finally admit our personal powerlessness, the space is created in which we begin to see how we are GIVEN power to act, think and feel. The greatest challenge in this is to recognize that we are empowered to act badly sometimes. Our awareness must expand considerably before we can recognize that even our selfishness and self-centeredness is given to us by the same Source that empowers us to act kindly and generously.

Once we begin to recognize that we are not independent droplets, that we are waves, inseparable from the great Ocean, self-centered fear naturally starts to evaporate. We become aware that whatever we do is a function of the Ocean as it expresses itself through the form and movement of us, the waves. All power is seen to originate in the Ocean and we, as waves, are simply expressions of that power, not controllers of it. Fear cannot survive in the environment of such awareness.

SEX

It is hard to imagine a more controversial subject than sex. It tops the list of most popular subjects that we rarely talk seriously about in public. With typical good sense the Steps take no position on it, other than to recognize that it is a natural human activity in which honesty is essential. The Living Teaching also refrains from taking a moral stance on the subject, but observes that it is the area of human activity in which there is often the greatest discrepancy between strongly held personal values and actual behavior. As such, it is fertile ground for a deeper look into the claim of personal power and control. Wouldn't we always do what we believe to be moral if we had the power to do so?

When we are unable to act in accordance with our moral principles, we call such lapses "moments of weakness," or think of ourselves as "weak." By this we mean we have some personal power, just not enough of it. From such a position, we compulsively continue on a lifelong and insatiable quest for more power and more control.

When will it end? When will we stop, take a look around and realize that the image of power and control we chase is a mirage?

One of the things we do in Step Four is to document our sexual history in writing, particularly as it relates to being dishonest, selfish or inconsiderate. We make sure to note any past sexual behavior for which we feel guilty or ashamed. Guilt and shame are red flags indicating the activity of the False Sense of Authorship. We feel guilty or ashamed only when we feel we had the power to behave properly and believe we chose not to. The Living Teaching encourages you to question the underlying assumption that you have personal power and discover if it is true.

GUILT AND SECRETS

The Fourth Step is the beginning of a process of cleansing that will continue through Step Ten. To this end, it is useful to include anything you feel guilty about, or continue harboring as a secret, that you have not yet listed with your resentments, fears and sexual history. The objective remains to be as honest as you can possibly be, holding back nothing, no matter how ugly or embarrassing.

WHO AM I?

Who am I? This is the ultimate question raised by Step Four, as well as of the Living Teaching. However, neither the Steps nor The Living Teaching answer the question for you. Both offer encouragement and guidance, but the task is yours to complete.

If you are clever, you might well ask me, "Who are you talking to? Who is the one you say is to complete the task?"

Sorry, I won't be tricked into giving you the answer. You will have to try to figure this one out for yourself!

May it find you now.

STEP FIVE

"Admitted to God, to ourselves, and to another
human being the exact nature of our wrongs."

Step Five is the important completion of Step Four. In
this step we share the information and insights from Step
Four with a trusted person. This offers an opportunity to
relieve the sense of isolation experienced when keeping a
portion of ourselves secret. It is, however, one of the most
frightening and difficult things some of us will ever do.
When we are able to push through the fear and take this
crucial step, the results are often quite spectacular. To
share our most intimate and closely held secrets about
who we are and what we've done (Step Four) with another person, is to shed a burden we may not even realize
we carry. This is particularly true in the area of sexual
behavior. Many of us come from societies in which sex,
outside of narrow, rigidly prescribed boundaries, is regarded as shameful, sinful or perverse. Many people
come to this point in the Steps with a sense that they are

"dirty" because of their past sexual behavior. It is remarkable how simply voicing our secrets to a trusted person (preferably one who has been through all the Twelve Steps themselves) can begin to free us from a lifetime of guilt and shame.

WELCOME TO THE HUMAN RACE

In Step Four, we began the process of getting honest with ourselves about who we actually are, as opposed to who we feel we SHOULD be. In Step Five, we take this honesty out into the world through admitting to another person who we are. This is the point at which we really start to come alive.

Trying to maintain a perfect vision of ourselves burns up an incredible amount of energy, whereas simply *being* what we are is effortless. Granted, we have imperfections (what the Steps call shortcomings and character defects), but as we will discuss in Steps Six and Seven, everyone has these. To be relieved of the burden of pretending to be something we are not is truly Grace.

The Fifth Step is a cleansing human ritual. Often, the person we ask to hear our Fifth Step also shares some of his or her own previously guarded secrets. In this way, the facade of independence, uniqueness and separation may thin or even fade completely away. We begin reconnecting to our own humanity. We realize we are part of something much bigger than our supposed independent selves. What an incredible relief! What extraordinary freedom!

For those fortunate enough to be able to participate in a Twelve Step group, the completion of Step Five is a major milestone. It is a rite of passage in which the initiate suddenly finds him or herself feeling part of the group. Even those of us who are not "joiners" may discover an appealing sense of kinship and connection with others who have experienced the freedom that inevitably comes with completing this Step.

The Big Book describes some of the reactions people have after sharing their personal inventory with another.

"We can look the world in the eye."[21]

"We can be alone at perfect peace and ease."[22]

"Our fears fall from us."[23]

"We begin to feel the nearness of our Creator."[24]

"We begin to have a spiritual experience."[25]

"We feel we are... walking hand in hand with the Spirit of the Universe."[26]

If you are reading this and have not yet actually taken the first five Steps, you are excused for imagining this is hyperbole. But if you have made it at least this far through the Steps, you likely have a taste of the feeling these phrases point to. There is liberation and freedom to be found in finally acknowledging the truth of who we are and by extension the truth of What Is. Where once we imagined we had to be *good* to feel worthy and complete, we now realize we need only be ourselves.

What an incredible relief!

May it find you now.

STEP SIX AND STEP SEVEN

6
"Were entirely ready to have God remove
all these defects of character."

7
"Humbly asked Him to remove our shortcomings."

Steps Six and Seven are nearly always discussed together. I have long suspected that they were originally one step that was split into two so there would be an even dozen.

Through more than seventy years and tens of thousands of Step study meetings, the battle rages over the difference between shortcomings and defects of character. For our purposes, I will talk about them as two terms pointing to the same thing with one very subtle difference. A defect of character is something that is present and can be easily recognized. A shortcoming refers to a quality that is absent and thus not so readily detected.

"Ram Tzu knows this.

You are perfect.

Your every defect
Is perfectly defined.

Your every blemish
Is perfectly placed.

Your every action
Is perfectly timed.

Only God could make
Something this ridiculous
Work"[27]

The essence of these two Steps is the continuing recognition of our own personal powerlessness. The Steps pointedly do NOT say that we begin working on correcting our shortcomings and defects of character. Trying to remove your own shortcomings is like trying to lift yourself off the ground by pulling on your own bootstraps while standing in your boots.

If you have read the Big Book you will have seen that the God it refers to is a masculine, objectified image of God, consistent with the culture and religious orientation of the book's writers. Some people today (including me) do not resonate with this image of God. Fortunately, these same writers do not insist we share their conception. The Steps are wonderfully spacious in this way. Each person can develop his or her own conception of what God is or isn't. Still, for some of us the language is off-putting. If you share this reaction, don't be discouraged. Many of us receive enormous value from the Steps and the Big Book while dancing around some of the more openly religious phrases and references. In my early days of working with the Big Book my antipathy to this term was so strong, I sometimes physically scratched out the word "God" and wrote in the words, "Infinite Unknown" in order to stomach some of the sentences. It may be worth mentioning that for me, this eventually passed. As my relationship with a Power greater than my egoic self grew, I found myself less reactive to the spiritual conceptions of others. I stopped seeking validation, agreement or even argument from others. It simply didn't matter how others put it; I began recognizing that these concepts were all pointers to the same thing. All that was important was my personal relationship with this, dare I say it, "God" of my own understanding.

In the Living Teaching of Advaita, God is not conceived of as an object. God, in Advaita, is the Ocean that is both the source and the substance of everything, yet is not a "thing" itself. As such, the Ocean cannot be known by the intellect because the intellect can only deal with objects. It is here that language fails us. Words can point to the ever-present Ocean, but words cannot describe the Ocean since it is not an object.

Many consider the Tao Te Ching to be the greatest text of nondualism. It begins with

"The Tao (Ocean, God) that can be told
is not the eternal Tao."[28]

Lao Tzu, the text's writer, acknowledges that what he writes about the Tao is not true in the absolute sense. But he doesn't stop there! He goes on writing beautifully about this Tao, all the while knowing that as soon as he writes about it, it isn't it. Taking my cue from Lao Tzu, I hasten to assure you that I make no claim that what I write is the Truth. With luck however, some of these pointers may find their mark in your heart and you will *see* what they point to. Or as Lao Tzu's cohort, Chuang Tzu said, "Show me a man who has no words, he is the one I want to talk to!"

In the Living Teaching, we utilize the Ocean metaphor to point to Consciousness. You'll recall that in this model, there is nothing other than Ocean. All things in the world are thus understood to be temporary, energetic movements of the Ocean — waves. We describe Ocean movement as waves, but a wave can have no independent existence from the Ocean. All that a wave is and does is totally dependent on the Ocean.

Within the context of Advaita, Steps Six and Seven point to an important understanding. We are not the individual creative entities we have always claimed to be. As such, we did not create our own shortcomings and defects, nor do we have the power to remove them.

Be warned, asserting such a thing publicly will likely invite a firestorm of contempt and derision from those convinced of their own power and independence. You will be accused of copping out, giving up, abdicating responsibility and a host of other negative things. Remember that we are not here to convince anyone else of anything. Our purpose is to find the Truth for ourselves. Such Truth is not to be found in debate with others, but through a deep and thorough investigation of who and what we are. As we see the Truth of What Is more directly, we move from belief to clarity. When firmly rooted in clarity, it no longer matters what others believe and say. What Is, simply Is.

True humility is the conviction that we are not the authors of ANY of our actions. Humbly asking God to remove our shortcomings is acknowledging our ultimate powerlessness.

When speculating about surrender, people often imagine that surrendering to a power greater than ourselves means we will do nothing. We will simply sit around all day waiting for God to act. That is not my experience, nor is it the experience of many others who go beyond speculation and actually take this path of surrender and inquiry. In fact, for most of us, the relief from the bondage of self that results from surrender energizes us, empowering us in ways we could never imagine.

One of the exercises in the Living Teaching is to write a list of the three most significant events in your life. Then consider to what degree you were responsible for creating these events. Most of us who do this exercise get a clear view of the important role Circumstance plays in our life. A genuine humility inevitably flows out of this recognition. The further implication is that had we been the one in control of our life, we would have short-changed ourselves.

ACCEPTANCE OF WHAT IS

It has been more than twenty-five years since I first took Steps Six and Seven. I wish I could report that all my shortcomings and defects of character are removed, but unfortunately that is not the case. As in the Ram Tzu poem above, all my flaws are divinely placed to make me the unique person I am today. We often imagine that freedom comes from no longer having shortcomings or defects of character, but this is a fantasy. Some of us have discovered that True Peace is found in Acceptance of things as they actually are in this moment, often including things we consider to be negative. I repeat, Acceptance does not suggest approval. Acceptance of things as they are is a simple but profound recognition of the state of things in this moment. This state of things *includes* our reactions and judgements.

When I first met my Teacher, Ramesh Balsekar, he often talked about Acceptance and personal powerlessness and since I was two years sober and had worked all Twelve Steps, I imagined I knew what he was talking about. He was unwavering in his assertion that Consciousness (Ocean) does everything and we (waves) are simply the expression of that doing. I had no difficulty with any of it since it was consistent with my understanding of the Steps. Yet, one day after attending his Talk, I went home and found my five year old son sitting on the floor doing something I had told him many, many times not to do! I became furious. I shouted at him, "Justin, I told you fifteen times not to do that and you keep doing it. What's the matter with you? You need a time out. Go to your room!!" He wandered off to his room, but I was left feeling as if I were the world's worst student of Advaita. It was as if I had forgotten all that I learned about how everything is actually being done by the Ocean. So the next day I went back to Ramesh's talk and admitted my failing. I told Ramesh the whole story of punishing my son as if he were responsible for the action and how I had forgotten that it was Consciousness that does everything. As I told the story Ramesh just sat there shaking his head and when I finished he said, "Wayne, what you forgot is that yelling at your son is the action of Consciousness too! Even when you think of Consciousness doing everything, you always leave your own actions out."

"If you can just Be, Be.
If not, cheer up and go on about other peoples business,
doing and undoing onto others 'til you drop!"
—E. E. Cummings

The freedom I know today lies in intuitively knowing that the Universe is in perfect order. This perfect order includes my own reactions, feelings and judgements, no matter how dysfunctional or unattractive they may be. As I am in this moment could not be otherwise and in the next moment, things *will* change.

It is the simplest of truths and one of the most profound. May it find you now.

STEP EIGHT AND STEP NINE

8
"Made a list of all persons we had harmed,
and became willing to make amends to them all."

9
"Made direct amends to such people wherever possible,
except when to do so would injure them or others."

The Steps come alive for me in their practicality. They recognize some very basic but profound principles of human life:

- The more you give, the more you get.
- Sharing your most intimate secrets with another brings freedom.
- When you clean up the messes you've made in your life, your life works better.
- Recognizing personal powerlessness is the doorway to the end of suffering.

While the Steps, particularly Steps Four through Ten, are eminently practical, their avowed goal is a spiritual awakening. The Steps give considerable attention to clearing away secrets and unresolved life messes because they can be particularly big blocks on the spiritual path.

It is difficult to live on earth for very long without making some messes. Those suffering from addictions inevitably harm friend and foe alike. Those without addictions also have shortcomings and defects of character that virtually guarantee they too harm others in some way, be it physically, emotionally or financially.

If we were rigorous and thorough in the Fourth Step inventory, we should have ample raw material to list all of the people we have harmed, which is the first part of Step Eight. Upon completion of this list, it is time to consider making amends. A vast storehouse of shared experiences on how to do this exists within the various Twelve Step groups. Every mistake that could possibly be made has already been made and freely talked about by someone (probably many people). You can potentially save yourself an immense amount of grief by consulting someone experienced in the amends process about what you plan to do *before* you do it.

While we gain personal freedom through making amends for the harm we brought to another, the Steps clearly point out that such freedom must not come at the cost of injury to them or others. You cannot assuage the guilt of being unfaithful by confessing to your unsuspecting husband that you slept with his brother but you are very sorry about it!

Usually, the most successful amends are those made after careful deliberation and forethought. Share your planned amends *in advance* with an experienced and knowledgeable person. Some people rush in enthusiastically and blindly only to report that their hoped for results don't come. Instead, they end up with a bigger mess than they started with.

To help foster willingness and to provide inspiration and encouragement in what is sometimes a difficult and frightening process, the Big Book describes the peace, comfort and calm that often results from engaging in internal housecleaning as outlined in Steps Four through Nine. These descriptions are collectively known as The Promises. Though I have watched them all come completely true in my life and the lives of many others, I do not believe there are any guarantees in life. The Promises listed below, are no exception. I have observed that they come in varying degrees and at different speeds to different people.

"We are going to know a new freedom and a new happiness.

We will not regret the past nor wish to shut the door on it.

We will comprehend the word serenity and we will know peace.

No matter how far down the scale we have gone, we will see how our experience can benefit others.

That feeling of uselessness and self-pity will disappear.

We will lose interest in selfish things and gain interest in our fellows.

Self-seeking will slip away.

Our whole attitude and outlook upon life will change.

Fear of people and of economic insecurity will leave us.
We will intuitively know how to handle situations
which used to baffle us.
We will suddenly realize that God is doing for us
what we could not do for ourselves."[29]

As I mentioned before, when I was about two years sober, the spiritual impetus of the Steps, combined with the desire to know the force in the Universe responsible for suddenly striking me sober, led me to a meeting with the spiritual teacher Ramesh S. Balsekar. Though I didn't suspect it when we met, he would become the single biggest influence in my spiritual development. For the next 22 years until his death in 2009, our lives were inextricably woven and I came to love him in a way that defies description.

Ramesh, upon retiring as the President of The Bank of India, actively resumed his lifelong interest in the subject of Advaita, eventually becoming a much published and much beloved teacher of the subject. Shortly after we met, there was occasion to share the Promises from the Big Book with Ramesh. He said they sounded like an excellent description of a person with profound spiritual understanding, a Sage. It was then that I began realizing the true universality of the principles pointed to in the Twelve Steps. They were as self-evident and true in Akron, Ohio as they were in Mumbai, India. The wording and cultural expressions were of course different, but the underlying principle of personal powerlessness was the same.

WILLINGNESS

Live as if your life depended on it.

–Ram Tzu

In Step Eight we once again face the question of willingness. As discussed previously, we cannot from our own power manufacture willingness, yet willingness must be there for us to proceed. Those who are religious are enjoined to ask God for willingness and if it is not immediately forthcoming, to keep asking. Those who are not religious may engage in a broad range of different strategies to increase willingness. One thing is certain: if there was a foolproof method to bring about willingness that worked all the time for everyone, we would have heard about it by now. Ultimately, we must recognize that willingness comes when it comes and we are powerless to make it happen.

The word "willingness" appears again and again throughout the Steps and it was one I had a lot of trouble with. How could these guys who wrote the Big Book keep harping on the idea that the presumption of self-will is the root of my troubles (which I could buy) and then turn around and tell me the solution to my troubles is through willingness?! It drove me crazy!

The difficulty was resolved during a talk by my dear teacher, Ramesh. He related a similar problem he had with his teacher of Advaita, a man by the name of Nisargadatta Maharaj. Nisargadatta would in one breath say "Consciousness (God) does everything, you do nothing." then in the next breath say, "In order for you to have a spiritual awakening you must be earnest. You must want it more than anything, like a drowning man wants air."

Ramesh said the apparent paradox of these two assertions made him go home and pull out his hair! How can he first tell me I do nothing, and then tell me I have to be earnest?

Ramesh said that he finally realized that his teacher was talking descriptively; describing that earnestness had to *happen* in order for the spiritual awakening to come. What Ramesh heard (through his own False Sense of Authorship) was a prescription for what he must do — to somehow make himself earnest. It became clear that a DEscription and a PREscription were two entirely different things.

When I began to see willingness as something that happened as Grace rather than something I had to make happen, all the tension went out of it.

The Big Book points to the same understanding:

> "We attempt to sweep away the debris which has accumulated out of our effort to live on self-will and run the show ourselves. If we haven't the will to do this, we ask until it comes."[30]

The asking certainly can't make the willingness come, but if the asking happens, it may be considered to be part of the coming. In looking back over my own experience with the Steps, it is clear that any willingness I had was pure Grace or "Unmerited Favor from God."

AMENDS

When it came time for me to make amends, I was reasonably well prepared but frightened. I owed a bar owner (who had made the expensive mistake of hiring me) quite a bit of money as a result of me frequently confusing my tip jar with the cash register. But even more frightening was that I owed my current business partner a LOT of money from several years of underpaying him what he was rightfully owed. I had to admit to him that I had betrayed his trust and cheated him. I feared he would sever our relationship and that I would be out of business.

I offered to pay the bar owner a fixed monthly amount that I could afford without bringing hardship to my family and he accepted. After several years, the debt was paid, and after the final payment I received a very nice note from him, telling me how much he ADMIRED me and he wished me well!

My business partner, to my surprise and relief, accepted my apology for having betrayed his trust and agreed to my proposal for returning what I had stolen. It took over six years, but in the end all the money was paid back. Our business together flourished and over the next dozen or so years he entrusted me with a great deal. This time his trust was not misplaced.

Amends such as these, while difficult and frightening at the time, are pretty straightforward. Sometimes it is impossible to make direct amends to the person we harmed and so we may need to get creative. One of the people on my amends list was someone whose name I never knew.

I was at a party on Dunk Island on the Great Barrier Reef in Australia and knocked a glass off a second floor railing. It broke on the ground below and I ignored it. A short time later a man screamed and then came in, bleeding severely. He had walked barefoot over the broken glass and had several severe cuts. I said nothing. When I got sober some thirteen years later in Los Angeles, the chances of finding this man and making amends to him were slim. The solution was a different kind of amends — a general, living amends. To this day, whenever I am somewhere where people are walking barefoot (like the beach or a park) and I see a piece of glass on the ground, I pick it up and take it to a trash can. It is a simple thing and yet every time I do it I get a small whiff of gratitude for all that my life has become.

I was able to make some living amends to my wife for the pain I had caused her, but our marriage did not survive. Not all amends bring the desired result. Nonetheless, we are friends today, and I can look her in the eye and know that through my amends, my side of the street is clean.

Nowhere is dramatic life change more evident than in the amends process. While there are no guarantees of positive results, stories of miraculous changes in damaged relationships and major reversals of fortune are commonplace. Nearly everyone who makes amends reports that they feel better about themselves and about life in general. The Promises are more than a sales pitch; they are a summary of what happens in the lives of those graced with the power to live by these spiritual principles.

May it find you now.

STEP TEN

"Continued to take personal inventory
and when we were wrong promptly admitted it."

For spiritual experience to flow smoothly, the channel
that carries it must remain clean and unblocked. Step Ten
is designed to maintain the clean channel created through
the completion of Steps Four to Nine.

Most of us are not saints, which is to say that our behavior is sometimes of a kind that neither serves ourselves nor others. With our growing understanding that
all behavior, both good and bad, is a product of Universal
Forces (Ocean) we remain free of guilt and pride. Remember that in Steps Six and Seven we reaffirmed that our
defects of character and our shortcomings were in God's
hands. Now to remain comfortable in life, we have to
quickly clean up any messes our character defects and
shortcomings may create.

CHANGE

At this point in our journey towards complete power-lessness, a disturbing question often arises: If we are powerless, can we change anything, or are we doomed to keep repeating the same mistakes over and over?

The answer is not so simple. As human beings we have desires and desire means change. If I have a head-ache, I will naturally want to change things so that I am no longer in pain. If I have a short temper that often gets me in trouble, I will naturally want to change so that my life is more trouble free.

We know from having lived our lives so far, that the only thing that is constant is change. Nothing in the en-tire universe is static. We know that change can and must happen, but when the FSA becomes involved, we lose sight of the Source of change. The activity of the False Sense of Authorship makes us feel as if we are ultimately responsible for making the change happen. Anxiety in-evitably follows. When the FSA is active, we have the im-pression that we are the one changing things. We claim that we author efforts in hopes of achieving the desired change. If the change DOES happen, the FSA then takes credit for bringing about the change. If the change does not happen, we (as the FSA) take the blame. But the same fundamental question applies: are we the authors of the change, or the agents through which the change occurs?

The tempting solution to this difficult question is to propose that we "co-author" change. This solution ac-knowledges forces bigger than us, but leaves us with the comforting sense of having at least SOME personal power. However, if we are rigorously honest in our inquiry, we must question the validity of this assertion of SOME personal power. Even if we decide we have it, where did we get it in the first place?

By this point, it almost goes without saying that we require what the Big Book calls "God's help" in order to have the power to do anything. If religious, we may ask God for help. If we are not religious, but grounded in the Living Teaching, we rest comfortably in the understanding that "God's help" will be forthcoming — or not. Realizing and accepting this "or not" is part of a deepening understanding and spiritual maturity. We don't always get what we want, or what we ask or pray for, or what we think we need or deserve. We get what we get.

Students of the Living Teaching are encouraged to recognize that whatever is happening or not happening in the moment is part of What Is. Many people mistake such an attitude as fatalism. It is not. Neither is it a New Age affirmation that everything that is happening is for the higher good. Rather it is a nudge toward an abiding peace in which there is the total absence of personal credit or blame for what happens. Implicit in such recognition is that change is inevitable. Just because things have been a certain way for a while — even a long while — does not necessarily mean they will continue that way.

Such understanding can be summed up with what I consider to be one of the wisest phrases ever penned: This too shall pass.

MISTAKES

As we continue the personal inventory in Step Ten, observing ourselves in ever changing situations, we will undoubtedly encounter mistakes. When the FSA is active and involved, we suffer when making mistakes. An interior dialogue takes place in which we berate ourselves for what we could have done and should have done differently. When the FSA does not claim to be the source of the action, there is an entirely different response to mistakes. When we make a mistake, there is still the recognition that we screwed up, but it is free from the sense "*I am* a screw-up." Our experience is that when we are not wasting energy beating ourselves up over the mistakes we inevitably make in life, we have far more energy available to clean up the mess the mistake has caused. This is the process of prompt and ongoing amends suggested in Step Ten.

The same principle applies to the mistakes of others. Our judgement is confined to their action and does not extend as a judgement of their worth as a person. This may seem like a subtle distinction, but it is actually quite profound.

Arrogance and insecurity are twin attributes of involvement by the FSA. Part of the FSA's claim of control is the claim of being right. Yet we are insecure because we know from a lifetime of experience that even when we are convinced we are right, we may be wrong. Often, we become defensive and stubborn. But as the claims of the FSA grow weaker through our ongoing practice of the Steps and through the inquiry suggested by Advaita, we can more readily admit when we are wrong.

We discover that being wrong is not the horrible trag-edy the FSA has made it out to be. We are not diminished by sometimes being wrong or making mistakes; we are simply human. We further find that when we admit to others that we are wrong, the other's defenses come down too. A space is created in which basic human connection and cooperation is far more likely to happen.

May it find you now.

STEP ELEVEN

"Sought through prayer and meditation
to improve our conscious contact with God as we
understood Him, praying only for knowledge
of His will for us and the power to carry that out."

Mention either prayer or meditation to someone and watch their brow furrow and their demeanor become serious. We have a lifetime of conditioning that communication with Source (God) is serious business. No smiles or laughter allowed!

But it needn't be this way. When prayer and meditation become totally integrated with daily life, both prayer and meditation can become quite light and joyous.

"As we go through the day we pause, when agitated or doubtful, and ask for the right thought or action. We constantly remind ourselves we are no longer running the show, humbly saying to ourselves many times each day 'Thy will be done.' We are then in much less danger of excitement, fear, anger, worry, self-pity, or foolish decisions. We become much more efficient. We do not tire so easily, for we are not burning up energy foolishly as we did when we were trying to arrange life to suit ourselves. It works–it really does."[31]

In the above, the Steps, ever practical, offer sound advice for those still struggling. Pause (if possible) and remember that it IS "Thy will" which is ALWAYS being done. Firmly rooted in such awareness, we cease struggling with What Is and know Peace regardless of what we find ourselves doing.

We benefit from a pause when agitated or doubtful because the agitation is usually the result of involvement by the FSA. Activity by the FSA distracts us from the task at hand. It is noisy and like an accident by the side of the road, almost impossible to ignore. When we pause, space and quiet usually follow. Clarity and inspiration often flows into the space created by the pause. Formal daily meditation is one kind of pause that can bring tremendous benefits. Even short, mini-pauses can be quite useful in keeping us from being swept into the maelstrom created by the FSA's incessant "shoulds." A few deep, focused breaths with eyes closed often does wonders. If you can remember, try it and see what happens!

Everything really does work a lot more easily and efficiently when we don't strain under the delusion that we are the masters of our own destinies and everything depends on us! Recognizing our personal powerlessness (that we are no longer claiming to be "running the show") is the unguarded secret to harmonious living.

Spiritual awakening is an understanding in which everything that happens in the universe can be described using one of two terms. For those things of which we approve or consider positive, we can describe with the term Grace. For those things of which we disapprove or consider negative, we can describe with the term God's Will. Both terms are potent pointers to the fact that everything that happens is a movement of the Ocean. The waves are not the authors of what they do, even though they sometimes claim to be.

When we begin to look into ourselves for the first time, we may suddenly realize that what is there is Ocean. This is a mind-expanding vision. Yet for most of us, this recognition of our Inherent Oceanness is experienced from the perspective of ourselves as a *droplet* of Ocean. Though still a limited vision, once we have this initial glimpse of ourselves as Ocean, there is no going back. Inevitably we bounce back and forth between feeling that we are separate droplets and feeling we are Ocean. The spiritual awakening, when it comes, is that we are not separate, independent droplets of Ocean that must reunite with the Great Ocean, nor have we ever been. We are nothing more and nothing less than the Ocean expressing as Life Itself.

Step Eleven is another one of those in which there is an interesting tightrope walk between religiosity and nondual understanding. The phrase, "praying only for knowledge of God's will for us and the power to carry it out," in Advaitic terms means we seek to recognize that all is God's will (the movement of the Ocean), and to be able to see that any power we waves possess to do anything, is God given — that all is a movement of the Ocean.

PERSONAL RESPONSIBILITY

No matter where 1 go in the world to talk with people about personal powerlessness, someone always asks, "What about personal responsibility? Can I act irresponsibly and if anyone objects just say that God made me do it?"

These questions are rooted in the assumption that we have the inherent power to create an action. It is precisely this assumption that lies at the root of our inquiry. Do we have this power? If so, do we control it? If we were able to control it, why would we act in ways that hurt ourselves and the ones we love? If you are able to look deeply into yourself as suggested in Step Eleven, you may find the answer to these questions.

Powerlessness is an Understanding, not an excuse. Once during talks in Vienna, a man came and brought his wife. When it was time for questions he excitedly raised his hand. "I am so glad you finally came to Vienna," he said. "I have brought my wife here so you can explain to her about how we are all powerless and that it is Consciousness that is responsible for everything. You see I like to have sex with other women, but she doesn't like this. I have tried to explain to her that it is the Ocean operating through me that makes me do what I do, but she doesn't understand. So please, maybe you could explain it to her better."

"I'll try," I said. "Your husband is correct that his sexual behavior is powered by a Force larger than his egoic self. He is either given the power to control his behavior or he isn't. With this understanding you cannot hate him for what he does. But your own reaction is powered by the same Force. The same Force that compels him to have sex with other women may compel you to leave him or to take a lover yourself or perhaps, even to kill him in a fit of jealous rage. No one can predict what will happen." Neither of them looked very happy with this answer and I never saw either of them again.

Our families, employers and the society we live in will continue to hold us accountable for our actions (or not). We may be rewarded or punished depending on how others evaluate what we do. The system is neither rigid nor fair. Sometimes our bad actions escape punishment and our good actions go unrewarded. Life plays by its own rules and they are ultimately too complex for the human mind to grasp. Some people believe fairness is restored in the afterlife or the next life. Complex systems of karma, heaven, hell and rebirth abound. Both the Living Teaching and the Steps remain resolutely out of such speculation. Perhaps the Buddha summed it up best when he said in the Lankavatara Sutra, "Events happen, deeds are done, but there is no individual doer thereof."

GOD CONSCIOUSNESS

The Steps refer to "conscious contact with God" which is a way of saying, "have a spiritual experience" or "glimpse our true nature." There are countless forms of spiritual practices designed to improve our "conscious contact." Part of the fun and excitement of the spiritual life is to wander around in the great spiritual marketplace. It is like exploring Istanbul's Grand Bazaar. There are thousands of merchants each enthusiastically proffering their wares. "Sir! Look at this treasure here sir! Over here sir!

Try this one! No, over here, this one is the best!" "Try some of this Tai Chi, Sir." "Hello, over here I have Centering Prayer." "Psssst, you want Tantra?" "Please sir, try my yoga in a hot oven." "Madame, have a look at this lovely Vipassana meditation." "Excuse me miss, would you care to try some lovely affirmations?" "Over here I have the finest Self Inquiry." "Sir!" "Madame!"

Yes, it can be overwhelming. Depending on your temperament, you may prefer the excitement of going it alone, or the sense of security that comes with having a guide. The important thing is to get out there and do it. Try this. Try that. There are sweat lodges and Bible studies, revival meetings and yoga classes. There are drum circles and sharing circles, labyrinth walks and pilgrimages of many kinds. See what suits you. When it comes to spiritual practices there is a near infinite variety, so if one doesn't feel right, simply try another one. Find one that seems interesting and see where it takes you. Take it easy. Relax if you possibly can. There is no requirement that you struggle, but if you do find yourself struggling, perhaps you will remember that it is the Ocean that is in movement as a struggling you.

When I began my own journey through the Grand Spiritual Bazaar, my objective was simple — to find power. I had recognized through the first Step that I was powerless over drugs, alcohol and a bunch of other things too. I had even conceded that in some ways I was limited in my ability to manage my life. My initial understanding of the Steps was that the solution lay in Spiritual Power and so I set out to get myself some — preferably a LOT! After all, the principle I had lived my life by was that more is better.

I was particularly interested in techniques that might help me align myself with God. I reasoned that with my brains and God's power, we could do great things together! Fortunately, I was able to get through that stage fairly quickly. There followed a series of spiritual practices and teachings that ranged from the sublime to the ridiculous. I learned something new from each one. The actual realization that I was TOTALLY powerless and all was playing itself out perfectly (including my liking it or not liking it) was to come later.

The creators of the Big Book observed, *"To some extent we have become God-conscious."*[32]

From the standpoint of the Living Teaching, this statement refers to a growing realization that we are not the independent entities we once considered ourselves to be. Rather, we are manifested aspects of the divine Self (Ocean). When we begin to know ourselves as waves rather than separate droplets, by definition we begin to know ourselves as Ocean. This is the God-consciousness or spiritual experience that the writers of the Steps point us toward.

God-consciousness is also the beginning of Self-awareness, which in the Living Teaching is sometimes referred to as "witnessing." We begin seeing ourselves and what we do in a new way. This witnessing is essentially impersonal. We are aware of ourselves, but not in the same self-critical way as before. We watch ourselves act and react. When we do something well, we delight in it without pride. When we do something unkind or dishonest, we regret it without guilt. From this perspective, we are far more likely to be able to quickly recognize performed actions requiring clean up (amends). Since there is less involvement by the FSA in this state, there is far less accompanying defensiveness and self-justification, all of which restrict us, robbing us of vitality.

Becoming "God conscious" also means we begin to grasp the difference between doing something and the sense of being the author of that doing. Waves "do," but only the Ocean "authors." When we know ourselves to be waves, we recognize that our actions, thoughts and feelings are the movement of the Ocean of which we are part. We no longer experience the suffering tied to the sense of personal responsibility for authoring our actions that we have when we consider ourselves to be powerful, independent entities (droplets). Increasingly, this awareness spreads from the intellect into the heart where it becomes fixed and permanent.

GOD'S WILL

The Big Book recognizes that even though you theoretically turned your will and your life over to the care of God in Step Two, you very likely still have at least some sense of personal will (FSA) left over. It says:

> "Every day is a day when we must carry the vision of God's will into all of our activities. 'How can I best serve Thee— Thy will (not mine) be done.' These are thoughts which must go with us constantly. We can exercise our will power along this line all we wish. It is the proper use of the will."[33]

We are faced here with a thorny problem. How can we exercise will (properly or otherwise) if we are truly powerless?

Most people first approach the Steps with the traditional thinking, "I am a separate, independent entity capable of self-will (a droplet)." Through the process of working the Steps, many people eventually gain insight and realize, "I am like a wave completely integrated with the Ocean that does everything." In order to speak to people at every stage of spiritual development, the Big Book walks a fine line between the two. In the beginning, there is usually tremendous uncertainty about how much of life is up to us to control, and how much is up to God to control. As we become increasingly aware of our true nature, the very idea of self-will becomes more and more nonsensical.

When I was first dealing with this question myself, I got a very good pointer from my friend and guide, Lee. We were talking about the Serenity Prayer, which says:

God grant me the serenity to accept the things I cannot change,
The courage to change the things I can,
And the wisdom to know the difference.

I couldn't figure out what I had to accept and what I had to change. Lee shared his own experience with this dilemma. He said he had taken a sheet of paper and drawn a line down the center. On one side of the line he listed the things he thought he could probably change. On the other side, he listed the things he thought he probably had to accept. He then put the list away and took it out again six months later and re-evaluated what he thought he could change and what he had to accept. Over several years he kept repeating the process. His observation was that items moved from the Things I Can Change side of the line over to the Things I Must Accept side, but that nothing ever moved the other way!

Once you admit you are powerless over at least one thing (as happens in the First Step) you become involved in a process that reveals itself to have a movement all its own. It is as if the FSA that claims to be a separate, independent "you" has a cancer. This cancer of Understanding gradually replaces the false "you" with itself until "you" are gone and only Understanding remains.

A huge benefit of the practicality of both the Steps and the Living Teaching is that they are not constrained by the same need for consistency, as are religions, philosophies and moralities. Though many people view the Steps with the reverence and immutability of scripture, the Steps are, in my view, simply excellent pointers and guides. They change as we change. Our growing and deepening understanding helps to illuminate aspects of the Steps and the Living Teaching that were simply invisible to us in the beginning.

THE SPIRITUAL PATH

You think of the Path
As a long arduous climb
Up the mountain.
You concede there may be
Many paths
But you're sure
All have the same
Exalted goal.

Ram Tzu knows this...

There are many Paths.

Like streams
They flow effortlessly
(though not necessarily painlessly)
Down the mountain.

All disappear
Into the desert sands below.[34]

The paths to obtain relief from the bondage of self are many and diverse. In India, the spiritual paths called "yogas" are divided into four broad categories. These are the path of Knowledge (Jnana), Devotion (Bhakti), Service (Karma) and Body/Breath (Hatha). Such paths correspond to the broad divisions in people's natures. These paths recognize that some people are predominantly intellectual, while others see life through their emotions. Others are service oriented and still others are more kinesthetic in nature.

It is important to remember that the various paths are not separate. The distinctions between them are purely notional, not actual. The mind, the heart, and the body are bound together as a seamless whole. Regardless of the path taken, the endpoint remains, "relief from the bondage of self." It is tempting to view this end to the bondage of self as something that is up to you to achieve. Both the Steps and the Living Teaching are here to remind you that, as with everything else, it is truly a matter of Grace. When this is forgotten and spiritual progress is claimed by the FSA as its own accomplishment, then spiritual pride (and the suffering that accompanies it) follows.

Our personalities draw us to different spiritual paths.

Extroverts are most often drawn to the paths of Action and Devotion while introverts tend towards the paths of Knowledge and Body/Breath. People who are emotional by nature tend towards the path of Devotion, while people who are more intellectual by nature, tend towards the path of Knowledge.

It should be noted that every one of us is a mixture of all these qualities. No one is exclusively this or that. Furthermore, no path is inherently better than another, though people who find themselves perfectly suited to a particular path often imagine that the path ITSELF is the perfect path. In acknowledging that there are different, equally valuable paths and seeing that it is our nature drawing us to a particular practice, we may be freed from the arrogance that can accompany finding the path that suits us.

RELIEF FROM THE BONDAGE OF SELF [35]

"When you understand the meaning of "Self" there will be no room for selfishness. Understand this thoroughly, abide in it, then in due course you will realize it. When the time is ripe, then it will happen." [36]

–Nisargadatta Maharaj

Spiritual awakening or spiritual experience can be defined as being relieved of the "bondage of self." To be relieved of the bondage of self is to realize that the self that claims responsibility for things is a phantom, it does not exist except in our unconscious imaginations. When this is first grasped, it is tempting to throw out the entire idea of being a self and begin to identify exclusively as Source, but with time and maturity, this proves to be unnecessary.

When we look into the question of self ever more deeply, we come to realize that what keeps us in bondage is not the self, per se, but the False Sense of Authorship that has hijacked the self, and subverted it. It is a subtle but crucial distinction and looking into this can save you a lot of awkwardness and grief. I can't tell you how many people over the years have visited me and proudly proclaimed that they are nobody!

ONE DAY AT A TIME

The collective wisdom embodied in the Twelve Steps can be summarized in the phrase, "One day at a time." Projection into the future is fodder for the FSA. Some part of us knows we lack sufficient power to control the future. As a result we grow fearful and either turn frantic with the sense we have to do *something* or we become immobilized. The sense we MUST control or the outcome will be negative puts us in a horrible position. It is like fighting a rip current. If you swim in the sea and find yourself carried out to sea by a rip current, the instinctual reaction is to attempt to swim directly back to shore. Unfortunately, it is impossible to overcome the strength of the current and you quickly grow exhausted while still being carried out to sea. The solution lies in swimming across the current since rip currents are localized phenomenon. If you do this, you will soon be out of it. Shifting your gaze from the future to what is happening now (living one day at a time) is a way to swim across the current. As we will soon discuss in Step Twelve, helping others when things are going badly for you is another effective way of swimming across the current. If you are blessed with the power to do either one, you will inevitably find yourself in calm water again and you will experience a kind of peace and well-being, even in difficult circumstances.

Perhaps the most famous and universally respected teacher of Advaita is Ramana Maharshi of South India. His Teaching captured the interest of Carl Jung who was also interested in the Twelve Steps because he considered alcoholism to be a "spiritual disease." Ramana Maharshi taught about realizing your own powerlessness through being still and asking yourself who you truly are (Self-Inquiry).

> "One of two things must be done: either surrender yourself, because you realize your inability and need a Higher Power to help you; or investigate the cause of misery, go into the Source, and so merge in the Self. Either way, you will be free of misery."[37]

Ramana acknowledges that for some people, prayer is a form of surrender in which the person who prays acknowledges their own lack of power by asking God for help. For others, he points to meditation as a form of investigation into what is the root cause of misery. Both paths can lead to the spiritual awakening discussed in Step Twelve.

> "The Power that created you has created the world as well. If It can take care of you, It can similarly take care of the world also... If God has created the world, it is His business to look after it, not yours."[38]
>
> –Ramana Maharshi

Upon reading such a statement, the FSA is likely to set off the "personal responsibility" alarm. Since the FSA claims to be the source of action it cries, "If I don't do it, nothing will be done. The world will be in even worse shape than it is. This is just another excuse for being lazy and neglectful." But Ramana is not suggesting that you should or that you even *could* spend your life sitting motionless and doing nothing. He is saying that if God needs something done, He will first put the thought to act in someone's mind and then give them all the energy and resources necessary to carry the action out. Where most people have difficulty with this concept is that it applies to everything, including the unpleasant stuff. Most of us, raised with the principle of self-will, were trained to picture God as the source of only the good. That usually leaves us, as separate individuals, holding the bag with all the bad. In the Living Teaching of Advaita, Ocean (God) is understood to be ALL. Therefore, good and bad are both contained within Ocean. Everything that happens is acknowledged as driven by the Ocean. The idea of a separate, independent entity capable of authoring good or bad acts is ultimately seen as an illusion.

SATSANG

Meetings of the Living Teaching are often called *satsangs*. *Satsang* is a Sanskrit word that means "a gathering in Truth." Within the *satsang* participants often feel a heightened connectedness (a conscious contact) with the Unifying Principle, God, Source, etc. This is an affirmation of the true order of things that is often obscured by the activity of the FSA. Twelve Step meetings also sometimes have this quality of *satsang*. It is a feeling rather than an idea. Beneath all the talk and the emotion is a unifying Essence, an intuitive sense that beyond our differences we are One. To abide in this sense is to live in peace.

> "In order to realize the miracle of what you Are,
> you must surrender the fantasy of what you will become."
>
> –Ram Tzu

It bears repeating that the Living Teaching is about living. Sometimes in the thrill and excitement of chasing Ultimate Understanding or Silent, Still Spaciousness, it is possible to lose sight of the miracles that abound all around us. Quite simply, life is amazing! But please don't take my word for this or ask me to elaborate on which things are so fantastic. Far better that you look for yourself. With Grace, this pointer will trigger something in you. Perhaps you will pause from reading this long enough to take a look around you or in you. Perhaps you will catch a glimpse of the underlying Unity of all things that is made manifest in all that you experience.

I can think of nothing more wondrous than walking the earth comfortable inside your own skin. This priceless gift accompanies the direct seeing of who and what you truly Are.

May it find you now!

STEP TWELVE

"Having had a spiritual awakening as the result of these Steps,
we tried to carry this message to alcoholics,
and to practice these principles in all our affairs."

When the Big Book first appeared, there was sufficient confusion about the terms "spiritual experience" and "spiritual awakening" to spur them into adding a clarifying appendix on the subject in the following edition. It is well worth reading. They make it clear that spiritual experience or awakening takes many forms. For some it is sudden and dramatic, for others, gradual and barely noticeable.

The Big Book also states,

> "Most of us think this awareness of a Power greater than ourselves is the essence of spiritual experience. Our more religious members call it 'God-consciousness'."[39]

The Living Teaching makes an important distinction between spiritual experience and spiritual awakening. We use the term spiritual experience to describe those moments that come and go in spiritual life during which there is an experience of the inherent unity of all things. It is the recognition that I and the other are One. The term spiritual awakening points to a permanent realization. It can be thought of as the death of the False Sense of Authorship, with no possibility of resurrection. This is the transcendent realization of a Unity that has always been and always will be. It is a Unity that is the container for time and the container for experience, yet is itself not a thing to be contained. (If that sounds like gibberish to you, don't worry, intellectual understanding is not the objective here.) Both spiritual experience and spiritual awakening come in their own time and when they do, all the words and explanations are recognized to be the feeble tools that they are.

The focus of the Living Teaching is to bring about a subconscious realization that we are integrated aspects of a Whole. With such preconscious awareness, we find ourselves in a state of acceptance of What Is. We cease struggling even when we are working hard to change something we don't like. It is truly the most blessed of human conditions.

THE DISAPPEARANCE OF GUILT

There is an assertion often made by people that feel guilt, that guilt is necessary to insure good behavior. They say that guilt inhibits us from acting badly. It is a peculiar argument because everyone knows from their own experience that they sometimes repeat the same behavior they previously felt guilty about. So even if it is an inhibitor, it isn't a very effective one. The experience of those of us who have actually had a spiritual awakening such that the FSA is dead and guilt no longer arises, is that there is no sudden increase in negative behavior. Unfortunately, there doesn't seem to be a sudden increase in positive behavior either!

I AM ONE WITH EVERYTHING— NOW WHAT?

Life is for living. Regardless of whether you have had a spiritual experience or a spiritual awakening, life goes on through this body and mind. We continue to eat, sleep, love, work, play, argue, fight, help, dance, laugh and cry in accordance with our natures and the dictates of the moment. It is very rare that we are converted into saints. However, the insights that come through the processes outlined in this book inevitably bring with them a reduction of selfishness and self-centeredness. Our hearts naturally open to others, particularly those struggling with the addictions or difficulties we previously faced. This is where Step Twelve directs us to share our "experience, strength and hope"[40] with those still suffering. Whether they suffer from an addiction or with the delusion that they are separate, independent and powerful entities responsible for creating a successful life, their burden may ease upon exposure to our direct experience and the positive transformation that usually accompanies the Teachings discussed in this book.

It is an observable pattern of human existence that when we help others without the expectation of reward, our own life is enriched. In Eastern tradition, this is known as karma yoga and the Twelve Steps are heavily weighted in this direction. Those of us who are also survivors of addictions are in a unique position to offer our genuine experience to others still suffering with that condition. This sharing is an amazing process, carrying strength and hope that somehow transfers to the other. Many of us have watched the miracle of recovery happen again and again. As a result, a rich tradition of sponsorship has developed within the various Twelve Step programs. Members of the group, who have ideally been through all or at least most of the Steps, freely share their experience on a one-to-one basis with someone new to the process. It is a genuine privilege to guide someone through this journey of recovery and self-discovery. When we selflessly give of our time and energy to help another come truly alive, we reaffirm the Grace in which we now live. That said, it is equally important to realize that the sponsor/sponsee relationship is subject to all the personal variances of any human relationship.

In the beginning, the relationship is inevitably unbalanced as the sponsor is the one with the experience, information, recovery and peace that the sponsee seeks. The greatest challenge for a sponsor in such a relationship is to resist the impulse to become an expert and to remain a sharer. The most successful of these relationships evolve into an incredibly intimate, balanced sharing between the two that enriches the lives of both participants, sometimes for a lifetime.

Nothing will put you in touch with personal powerlessness like working with others. You will notice that this step says we "tried" to carry the message. By this point in the process, it is hopefully clear that we do not have the personal power to bring about a result. We can try to carry the message, but the success or failure of our efforts is not in our hands. As they say in AA, "We don't get 'em sober and we don't get 'em drunk."

SHARING OUR EXPERIENCE

There is a monumental difference between sharing our own experience with others and telling people what we believe to be true. Firstly, no one can argue with our experience. When we genuinely share our experience, our listeners' alarm bells don't go off as they do when they get the feeling that we are trying to change their beliefs or trying to convince them that our opinions are correct.

The Big Book says:

> "Unless one's family expresses a desire to live upon spiritual principles we think we ought not to urge them. We should not talk incessantly to them about spiritual matters. They will change in time. Our behavior will convince them more than our words."[41]

This is truly an enlightened insight. It applies equally to friends and co-workers. Allow who you have become to do the talking for you. This may take some time and patience on your part, but when others observe a positive change in you, they may well approach you in a spirit of open curiosity. When someone approaches you with sincere interest and curiosity, they are much more likely to be receptive to hearing of your experience. After all, the proof of what you share stands right in front of them. They have already noticed it or they wouldn't have asked you about it in the first place. There is no need to proselytize. We are not trying to build a religion or a philosophical or social movement. We seek only to learn to live comfortably in our own skins by discovering our true nature and then sharing it through our presence and our deeds. This principle of "attraction rather than promotion"[42] is fundamental to the Twelve Step programs and applies equally to the insights gained through the Living Teaching.

We share our experience because we have seen it is the most efficient way to communicate what we've learned. Telling people what we think we know just doesn't work. But everyone enjoys a story. And our experience is the story we know best. It is easy to tell and easy to listen to. The magic is that even if the listener has not shared our experience, some of the truth of our experience gets transferred through the story.

Wherever and whenever this insight is genuinely communicated, it remains free from end-gaining, belief, path, opinion or process. What we have discovered cannot be taught, but it is continuously shared. Because it is our inheritance, no one can claim ownership of it. It need not be argued, proven or embellished. It stands alone simply as it is. Hopefully, at this stage we are fully convinced that we do not control the results of our efforts. Whether the insight we share goes unrecognised or is rejected, or becomes realized and lived, we know is not in our hands.

Talking with people and sharing experiences is easy for extroverts. Yet we also see introverts and loners finding comfort in their association with others, particularly when the relationship is grounded in acceptance. After all, we are inextricably connected, one to the other as waves, and therefore Ocean. Some deep part of every human being recognizes this.

In Step Twelve, we are exhorted to abandon the false sense of separation by paradoxically helping others. In doing so we come to realize that the other is NOT separate. To help the other is to help ourselves.

THE WAVE IS THE OCEAN

With a spiritual awakening, we realize the full Unity of the wave and the Ocean. A surprising feature of this realization is that the waves haven't disappeared. In fact, the waves, be they beautiful or ugly, kind or mean, gentle or violent are all magnificent, complex expressions of Ocean. We come to understand that all of the qualities, actions and reactions of the waves (me and the other) are also expressions of Ocean. The burden of pride and guilt, carried since the age of two years old, slips from our shoulders as if it had never existed.

To operate as if we have the personal power to control and make things happen is to usurp the power of God (Ocean). It is the ultimate blasphemy. When we give up this false claim, when we "stop playing God," remarkable changes occur. The writers of the Big Book describe their experience like this:

> "More and more we became interested in seeing what we could contribute to life. As we felt new power flow in, as we enjoyed peace of mind, as we discovered we could face life

successfully, as we became conscious of His presence, we
began to lose our fear of today, tomorrow or the hereafter.
We were reborn."[43]

Perhaps you have noticed the amazing paradox; as we
recognize our inherent personal powerlessness, "new
power flows in." Part of the false claim of personal power
is that without it, we will sit around doing nothing. At best
we will be suited only for sitting in a mountain cave, being
chewed on by rats (we won't care) and dispensing spiritual wisdom to seekers intrepid enough to find their way to
us. Our collective experience is that this *is a false fear*. Once
we know ourselves to be Ocean in the form of wave, we
become free to be ourselves in a way we never dreamed
possible. It is as if we had spent our life driving with the
emergency brake on and suddenly it is off.

Step Twelve urges us to practice these principles in all
our affairs. Of all the principles, none is more important
than the recognition of personal powerlessness. When we
recognize personal powerlessness in our own actions, the
twin burdens of pride and guilt vanish. When we recognize powerlessness in the actions of others, it frees us from
the poisoning effects of resentment and hatred. Relieved
of pride, guilt, resentment and hatred, we live comfortably
with life as it comes, in true humility and peace. We finally
recognize Who and What we truly are.

May it find you now.

A CONVERSATION WITH GOD

I have a plan,

(God chuckles)

Why do you laugh?

Because I know you have a plan.

You do?

Of course, where do you think your plan came from?

You're responsible?

Yes, for everything.

Everything?

Everything.

I thought I have free will...

I know.

You know?

Yes, where do you think that thought originated?

You're claiming that also?

Yes, everything.

But wait, I have the power to choose. For example I can choose whether to believe in you or not.

I know, that was one of my more clever ones — if I do say so myself. I especially like the part where you change what you believe to the exact opposite.

I am beginning to think you are a sadist.

Perhaps, but after all I am your creation.

My creation? I thought I was your creation.

I know.

THE END IS THE BEGINNING

In a moment of supreme Grace we come to the realization that we suffer from the most insidious kind of addiction — the one we don't even realize we have. It is the addiction to power itself. We seek to control life despite the fact that all our efforts to control end in misery. We persist as relentlessly as any addict, pursuing peace and relief in the chimera of personal power. Always it eludes us. We insanely repeat the same behavior over and over with the hope of a different result. By any other name this is addiction. There is only one way out and that is through. We are back at the First Step. We admit we are powerless over our addiction to control. The First Step more than any other is the key to recovery. Whenever we feel lost, confused or fearful, we can return to the refuge of the First Step and be renewed.

POWER RETURNS

The enduring paradox and wonder of a spiritual awakening is the return of power. But this power has a completely different feel to it. It is impersonal. Without the bondage of self, the power of the Ocean plays out without resistance. All our actions as waves flow with liquid harmony. The rapturous spiritual poets liken this to the ecstatic feeling of love, which is powerful and transformational and totally beyond any possibility of personal control.

It is always tempting to soar with the angels. After all, pleasure, joy and fulfilment are easy to accept. What has always attracted me to both the Steps and Advaita is that they ground us in life as it is. Soaring with the angels may indeed be part of that, but life is richer and fuller when freed from the fantasy that life can somehow take the form of a single ended stick. Can you imagine a stick with only one end? Probably not, since in this Universe all sticks have two ends. Yet, fantasizing a life in which there is only good and no bad, only joy and no sorrow, only pleasure and no pain is fantasizing about having a single ended stick. Of course we prefer beauty to ugliness and happiness to sadness. But when we shut our eyes and hearts to the negative aspects of life, we fall back into delusion. It is almost irresistibly tempting to try to escape the negative and try to have only the positive. But believing this is possible and living in the vain hope that someday, perhaps even in some future lifetime, you will achieve a life without anything negative in it, is trading in living for dreaming. When you compare life as it is to a fantasy ideal of perfection, the life you live inevitably falls short and you suffer. You are left with the horrible sense that things SHOULD be different than they are in this moment. It is the most damning of beliefs.

The New Age/self-help solution is to try to recast the negative, difficult things as positive. We are told that it is all good, even the bad is good, and we need only adjust our perception in order to transform the bad into the good. This may work for a time, but those of us who have tried it for a while have seen that such mind tricks ultimately fail in the end.

With a spiritual awakening we recognize that positive and negative are connected, each contains the seed of the other. We see the underlying harmony that is the Ocean, but it doesn't wipe the opposites out, nor does it convert them into singular positivity. With the awakening to the underlying Unity of all things comes a powerful Acceptance of all that is — we experience the bad along with the good and know that they are inexorably linked.

TRANSCENDENCE

We come to the end and yet remain at the beginning. This is the realm of mystics. All is exactly as it has always been, and yet, is radically different. The false claim of power is gone. In complete powerlessness, we are simultaneously more and less than we previously imagined ourselves to be.

Upon waking to fundamental Unity, the things of the world are stripped to their essence. All those people and events once appearing as separate and independent are revealed to be integrated — waves that are part of a vast Ocean. The waves have not disappeared — there is no need for them to disappear, as their presence (no matter how unpleasant or discordant) cannot disturb the Wholeness. This is Transcendence. The many and the One peacefully coexist. The apparent rift is miraculously healed.

Spiritual poets and songwriters throughout history have rhapsodized about spiritual awakening such that a rich folklore and mythology has grown up around it. It is often associated with ecstasy and bliss and supernatural powers. The people through whom awakening has happened are often venerated and some become spiritual teachers. If part of an organized group, they are ascribed the highest values of the group and upon death, often become legends and symbols. You have to admit, it is all very exotic, exciting and attractive.

As a matter of personal preference, I talk about this spiritual awakening in more down-to-earth terms. I suppose this is not so surprising when you consider my history in the bars and drug houses of the world rather than the temples and ashrams. Furthermore, my guru was a banker not a cave dweller!

My experience and vision is one in which life is understood to be a vast and complex happening — a perfect expression of an incomprehensible Wholeness that is what I am. Events and my experience of them help to comprise this Wholeness. I know myself to be BOTH immanent and transcendent. I am Wayne and I am God. I am God, not because I am special or unique, but because EVERYTHING is God. I am uniquely special and at the same time, I am undifferentiated Wholeness. All my imperfections are perfectly placed. I sometimes act badly, but I am incapable of sin. I am everything and nothing. I was born (and will die) and yet I am Eternal. I have no personal power and I am Power itself. Nothing I know or believe is true and

Truth is all I ever was or ever will be. I drank myself to death and was resurrected as the Guru. The world at large thinks me crazy and of course they are right. What most people consider ordinary, I see as miraculous. I am no longer rational in the traditional sense. I make sense only to those who are touched by my madness. I am reliable and subject to unexpected change at any moment. I walk around appearing to be normal, but I inhabit a world known to only a few. I sometimes work hard to get what I want, always knowing that I am powerless to make anything happen. I am at peace when I am angry. I love even those I dislike the most. My disapproval is grounded in Acceptance of all that IS. I am not afraid to die because I know myself to be Life itself. I weep over my losses even though I have never had anything and never will have anything. All is UNDERSTOOD in perfect clarity and I don't really know a damned thing. I consume the suffering of others, yet I do not suffer. My heart is attached to a pacemaker and it still beats in rhythm with the Universe. Love fills me to the point where I am completely empty. I always tell the Truth even when I lie. I remain fulfilled though my desires are frequently not met. I expect nothing and am often furious when I don't get what I want. I make no promises or guarantees, but I am trustworthy. You can count on me for nothing.

All the apparent paradoxes of the world dissolve in this simple Understanding. This is Acceptance of What IS. This is Peace. This is Transcendence.

May it find you now!

"We shall not cease from exploration and the end
of all our exploring will be to arrive where we started.
And know the place for the first time."

-TS Elliot

ACKNOWLEDGEMENTS

I have dedicated this book to the men at Scotty's/ Splash, some of whom I have been privileged to know for more than twenty-five years, but were it not for the ongoing support of two very special women I would surely have floundered.

My beloved wife Jaki Scarcello bears the full brunt of God's reluctance to remove all my shortcomings and defects of character. Her loving presence in this crazy, beautiful life we live is the greatest of blessings. I am beyond grateful for her support.

Dawn Salva is Source's gift to both me the writer and you the reader. Her sensitivity and skill as an editor and her deep understanding of the subject have added immeasurably. Her boundless love hasn't hurt matters either.

My dearest and oldest friend Bill Cleveland has walked with me for a long time. He is a tireless karma yogi, fully dedicated to the path of service. His insights are to be found scattered throughout this book though I'll be damned if I'll give him credit for any of them.

Lee Scantlin has also been in on this heist since the beginning. His entry into my life was the catalyst for the evolution that followed and several of his insights inform these pages.

Many thanks also go once again to Nacho Fagalde for his ongoing love and support for me and the Living Teaching. Much of the work on this book was done in the quiet, peaceful space he so generously provided.

Steven Hoel, Tall Kathy, Rambo and Bala all warrant special thanks for their feedback in the formative stages of the manuscript. Proofreaders JoAnne Franz Moore, Heidi Singfeld and Lee Scantlin were invaluable in finding the typos, and reinforcing my conviction that punctuation is an art not a science (Who thinks there should be a comma after typos? Raise your hand).

I particularly want to thank the Advaita Fellowship and all the members who financially support it for keeping us fed, clothed and housed. It is a suspicion amongst detractors that I am getting rich and fat off the Teaching and while I may be getting fat, the rich part remains the remotest of possibilities.

And last but certainly not least, there is Rebecca, who helps bring some much needed order to my chaos.

Oh yes, and Leonard, thanks for the tickets.

ENDNOTES

1. *Alcoholics Anonymous,* 3rd edn (New York City: Alcoholics Anonymous World Services, Inc. 1976-2001), p. 88.

2. ibid.

3. *Alcoholics Anonymous,* 4th edn (New York City: Alcoholics Anonymous World Services, Inc., 2001-12), p. 164.

4. ibid., p. 61

5. ibid., p. 30

6. ibid., p. 31

7. ibid., p. 59

8. ibid., Foreword to Fourth Edition, p. xxiv

9. ibid., p. 45

10. ibid., p. 46

11. ibid.

12. ibid., p. 60

13. ibid., p. 62

14. ibid.

15. ibid.

16. ibid., p. 58

17. ibid., p. 62

18. ibid., p. 64

19. ibid., p. 68

20. *Alcoholics Anonymous,* 4th edn (New York City: Alcoholics Anonymous World Services, Inc., 2001-12), p. 83

21. ibid., P. 75

22. ibid.

23. ibid.

24. ibid.

25. ibid.

26. ibid.

27. Ram Tzu, aka Wayne Liquorman....*No Way for the Spiritually Advanced*, Advaita Press, 1990 pp 47

28. *Tao Te Ching*, Translated by Gia-Fu Feng and Jane English, Vintage Books Edition, 1989 pp 3

29. *Alcoholics Anonymous*, 4th edn (New York City: Alcoholics Anonymous World Services, Inc., 2001-12), pp. 83-84.

30. *Alcoholics Anonymous*, 4th edn (New York City: Alcoholics Anonymous World Services, Inc., 2001-12), p. 76

31. ibid., pp. 87-88

32. ibid., p. 85

33. ibid., p.63

34. Ram Tzu, aka Wayne Liquorman....*No Way for the Spiritually Advanced*, Advaita Press, 1990 pp 94

35. *Alcoholics Anonymous*, 4th edn (New York City: Alcoholics Anonymous World Services, Inc., 2001-12), p. 63

36. Nisargadatta Maharaj, edited by Jean Dunn, *Prior To Consciousness*, Acorn Press, p. 154

37. Ramana Maharshi, ... *Spiritual Teaching of Ramana Maharshi*, Shambhala, p. 67

38. ibid., p. 64

39. *Alcoholics Anonymous*, 4th edn (New York City: Alcoholics Anonymous World Services, Inc., 2001-12), Appendix II, p. 568.

40. Copyright by The AA Grapevine, Inc.

41. *Alcoholics Anonymous*, 4th edn (New York City: Alcoholics Anonymous World Services, Inc., 2001-12), p. 83

42. ibid., The Twelve Traditions, p.562

43. ibid., p. 62

MORE FROM ADVAITA PRESS

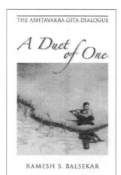

A DUET OF ONE
by Ramesh S. Balsekar

Here Ramesh uses the Ashtavakra Gita as a vehicle for an illuminating look at the nature of duality and dualism.

Softcover
224 Pages
$16.00

WHO CARES?!
by Ramesh S. Balsekar

This is the boook we recommend to those asking for a book that will describe the essence of Ramesh's teaching. Ramesh's ability to cut through to the simple heart of complex ideas is a joy to experience.

Softcover
220 Pages
$16.00

ACCEPTANCE OF WHAT IS
by Wayne Liquorman

A look at Advaita through the eyes of the most unlikely of Sages. Wayne's expression of his spiritual understanding is at once irreverent and profound. We laugh, sometimes joyously, sometimes uncomfortably but always with the recognition that we are in the presence of a Master.

Softcover
304 Pages
$16.00

YOUR HEAD IN THE TIGER'S MOUTH
by Ramesh S. Balsekar

A superb overview of the Teaching. Transcribed portions of talks Ramesh gave in his home in Bombay during 1996 and 1997.

Softcover
472 Pages
$24.00

A NET OF JEWELS
by Ramesh S. Balsekar

A handsome bedside volume of jewels of Advaita, selections from Ramesh's writings presented in the format of twice daily meditations.

Softcover
384 Pages
$25.00

NEVER MIND
by Wayne Liquorman

Take a revealing and inspiring journey into the heart of Non-dualism. Wayne's Teaching is presented here with clarity and sophistication. A most welcome addition to the spiritual library.

Softcover
174 Pages
$17.00

RIPPLES
by Ramesh S. Balsekar

A brief and concise introduction to Ramesh's Teaching. Perfect to give to friends.

Softcover
44 Pages
$6.00

NO WAY FOR THE SPIRITUALLY ADVANCED
by Ram Tzu

No Way is a unique blending of wit, satire and profound spiritual insight. One minute we are howling with unconstrained laughter, the next we are squirming in self-conscious recognition as Ram Tzu holds up a perfect mirror and then gleefully points out that we aren't wearing any clothes.

Softcover
112 Pages
$13.00
Also available on Audio Cassette $15.00

ENLIGHTENMENT IS NOT WHAT YOU THINK
by Wayne Liquorman

Many consider it to be Wayne's best book yet. It helps dispel the illusion that Consciousness is something other than who you already are.

Softcover
228 Pages
$19.00